REAL REVIVAL PREACHING

REAL REVIVAL PREACHING

Bailey E. Smith

BROADMAN PRESS
Nashville, Tennessee

© Copyright 1982 • Broadman Press
All rights reserved
4262-35
ISBN: 0-8054-6235-X

All Scripture verses are from the King James Version of the Bible.

Dewey Decimal Classification: 269.24
Subject heading: REVIVAL SERMONS
Library of Congress Catalog Number: 81-86667
Printed in the United States of America.

DEDICATION

This book is dedicated to Michael Haynes, pastor, author, scholar, and gifted interpreter of the Word of God. He and his Priority Ministries have been a great blessing to my life and ministry.

Contents

1. Trees That Testify 9
2. The Worth of the Work 21
3. Five Fruitful Failures 29
4. The Result of Revival 43
5. The Battle of Building 55
6. Revival or Regret 65
7. Four Things God Does Not Know 75
8. The Gospel in Miniature 89
9. A New Commitment to an Ancient Commission 97
10. Characteristics of a Dynamic Church . 109
11. Echoes of Encouragement 121
12. Let the Church Stand Up in Today's World 129
13. Hour of Decision 139

1
Trees That Testify

Let's for a moment think about trees in the Bible. In Luke 19 there is mention of a certain tree. Most people have known about that tree since childhood. Many will identify with every tree in this chapter, and some will relate to one or two. But I trust that at least two of these trees will be essential to you.

Trees are interesting. When my family moved to Hobbs, New Mexico, I asked my wife if she thought the Lord was calling us to that state. She replied, "No, there are no trees." She's from Arkansas where there are large beautiful trees, and in Hobbs there were no trees, no bridges, and not much water.

I remember reading about a city in Wisconsin where a courthouse was going to be built. There was a furor over whether a huge maple tree would be cut down or not. All kinds of people drew up a petition, saying a courthouse could not be built at that particular location because the engineer and landscapers had stated that the maple tree would have to go. Finally, the rebellion of the people was so strong that they decided to leave the maple tree, and literally built the courthouse around the tree!

Did you read about the lady who stood by a cottonwood tree with a shotgun and threatened to kill anyone who cut on her tree? That's what I call loving a tree.

People love the shade and the luxuriant growth of trees.

There is a majestic quality about a tree. I suppose that God loved a tree. "Poems are made by fools like me," wrote Joyce Kilmer, "but only God can make a tree." There are seven important trees from which we can learn vital lessons.

THE SYCAMORE TREE

In Luke 19 the sycamore is seen as the tree of salvation.

> And Jesus entered and passed through Jericho. And, behold, there was a man named Zacchaeus, which was the chief among the publicans, and he was rich. And he sought to see Jesus who he was; and could not for the press, because he was little of stature. And he ran before, and climbed up into a sycamore tree to see him: for he was to pass that way. And when Jesus came to the place, he looked up, and saw him, and said unto him, Zacchaeus, make haste, and come down; for to day I must abide at thy house. And he made haste, and came down, and received him joyfully. And when they saw it, they all murmured, saying, That he was gone to be guest with a man that is a sinner. And Zacchaeus stood, and said unto the Lord; Behold, Lord, the half of my goods I give to the poor; and if I have taken any thing from any man by false accusation, I restore him fourfold.

I believe that man was saved. When a person comes to know Christ, it not only gets him into heaven, but it gets heaven into him. Here Zacchaeus testified, "Lord, if I have done one thing wrong, I want to restore it fourfold."

It's amazing how when a person is saved, he puts his past behind him. If you have had a wicked past, or if you have been lying, cheating, committing adultery, or stealing, whatever, you should do everything you can to straighten up your past. True, the blood of Jesus will carry you to heaven. True,

the blood of Jesus has made your sins to be cast as far as the east is from the west, but if you can make some restoration, you can give those years of your life to the church in greater quality to make up for those years when you were living for the devil.

Zacchaeus said, "I will restore." If you please, "I will make restitution." The sycamore tree of salvation is interesting to me. What is your sycamore tree? What tree were you in when you found Jesus? I was in Elam Road Baptist Church in Dallas, Texas. A man in that church preached on hell five nights in a row. The fifth night the Holy Spirit convicted me. I was ten years of age. The sycamore tree from which I found Jesus was the Elam Road Baptist Church where my father was pastor. What is your sycamore tree?

To some people over at First Southern Baptist Church "Starlight Crusade" was their sycamore tree. To some it is their own church—to others a revival meeting. Zacchaeus came to see Jesus because of curiosity. He had heard about all that Jesus Christ was doing, and he wanted to see Jesus. Many people come to our services out of curiosity, but then they find the way of life.

Zacchaeus came out of curiosity. The reputation of Jesus had gone around and Zacchaeus couldn't stand it anymore. He had heard about people who had been blind, but could now see. He heard about cripples walking. He even heard about a dead man being returned to life.

Look around you. See the lives that are changed. See the prostitutes who are now virtuous women. Look at the dope addicts who are now whole. See the alcoholics who are now sober. See the depressed who have found a new joy in life. Look around you and you will see the footsteps of Jesus.

The only problem with a sycamore tree is that many people fall in love with it and they never move. They lie under the shade of that tree and never move. They walk down the aisle and someone hands them a card and instructs, "Fill this out

and sit here." And the misguided convert thinks that is the Great Commission. They've been sitting ever since.

The sycamore tree is only to help you start; it's not designed to keep you in the shade.

The Bible states that as Zacchaeus looked down from that tree he began to fall under conviction. When he really saw Christ, he said, "Lord, I'll begin to restore things." This was the first time in his life that Zacchaeus had seen cheating in all its rottenness, because this was the first time in his life that Zacchaeus had viewed sin as God sees it. He could no longer stay the crooked businessman he had always been. He had to restore himself.

Can you imagine seeing a man mercilessly beating a little child and doing nothing about it? Even a human instinct would make us try to prevent that man from doing that. You would be so repulsed by that because your standard of morals and ethics are higher than that. My dear friend, God is fully as repulsed by everything that is sinful. There is not one sin you have that does not repulse God. This includes pride, arrogance, lying—whatever it is, to God it is repugnant. I pray that as Zacchaeus came under the conviction of his sin when he saw Jesus, that we could see our sins as God sees them.

Sin barks out, "I want to do what I want to do when I want to do it." That's the sure sign of a person on the road to the devil's hell. Find the sycamore tree of salvation and see sin as God sees it.

THE OAK TREE

The next tree is the oak tree. This is the tree of disobedience. Notice 1 Kings 13:14 ff.:

> And went after the man of God, and found him sitting under an oak: and he said unto him, Art thou the man of God that camest from Judah? And he said, I am. Then he said unto him, Come home

with me, and eat bread. And he said, I may not return with thee, nor go in with thee: neither will I eat bread nor drink water with thee in this place: For it was said to me by the word of the Lord, Thou shalt eat no bread nor drink water there, nor turn again to go by the way that thou camest. He said unto him, I am a prophet also as thou art; and an angel spake unto me by the word of the Lord, saying, Bring him back with thee into thine house, that he may eat bread and drink water. But he lied unto him. So he went back with him, and did eat bread in his house, and drank water. And it came to pass, as they sat at the table, that the word of the Lord came unto the prophet that brought him back: And he cried unto the man of God that came from Judah, saying, Thus saith the Lord, Forasmuch as thou hast disobeyed the mouth of the Lord, and hast not kept the commandment which the Lord thy God commanded thee, But camest back, and hast eaten bread and drunk water in the place, of the which the Lord did say to thee, Eat no bread, and drink no water; thy carcase shall not come unto the sepulchre of thy fathers. And it came to pass, after he had eaten bread, and after he had drunk, that he saddled for him the ass, to wit, for the prophet whom he had brought back. And when he was gone, a lion met him by the way, and slew him: and his carcase was cast in the way, and the ass stood by it, the lion also stood by the carcase. And, behold, men passed by, and saw the carcase cast in the way, and the lion standing by the carcase: and they came and told it in the city where the old prophet dwelt. And when the prophet that brought him back from the way heard thereof, he said, It is the man of God, who was disobedient unto the word of the

> Lord: therefore the Lord hath delivered him unto the lion, which hath torn him, and slain him, according to the word of the Lord, which he spake unto him.

The Bible continues to declare that the donkey stood right there with the lion, and the lion didn't even try to eat the donkey. The donkey and the lion stood looking at this dead preacher the lion had killed. The donkey didn't want to eat him. Then the prophet came and took the old dead preacher and put him on the donkey and took him back into town and put his body into a strange tomb.

This is the story of a preacher who listened to man rather than God. It was the oak tree of disobedience. I want to promise you something. As long as God gives me enough sense to know what I am doing, I will desire with all of my heart not to preach what man wants me to preach, but what the Bible has for our generation.

When this preacher in the story began to listen to another preacher, he fell in trouble. It cost him his life.

Are you listening to voices other than God? Right now, some are dwelling under the oak tree of disobedience. Often education merely makes a more clever devil. Don't listen to the voice of education without Jesus Christ, because education without Jesus Christ can make you an intellectual fool.

It's amazing how many voices we want to listen to. I am astonished sometimes at how dumb girls and boys are. I realize we are living in a time of "liberated women," but I am floored by the dumb girls I am seeing lately.

A young girl said, "He promised that if I would move in and live with him, he'd take care of me. Now he's leaving me. I don't have anywhere to go." I said, "Why shouldn't he? He's got what he wanted. He wanted you for a playmate, not a friend."

Girls, you are being so foolish. These young men talk to you about "trial marriage." That will not work. They don't

want it to work because they can use you and then take what's left of you and throw you out. Then they'll go find someone "fresh."

It doesn't matter how delightful or charming he seems, his only intention is to use you for his pleasure. You had better be careful. God's Word teaches us to be pure. The world says, "You can let down your standards." Oh! Don't listen to some playboy when you can listen to God. It will cost you something precious.

And many a young man is drawn in and trapped by an enticing woman who has the morals of a black widow spider. When that man climbed under the oak tree of disobedience, it cost him his life. Sometimes your friends are wrong. I know so many people who go to work and sit behind expensive desks. Then, they go to the bar, and then home to fuss at their wives. Then, they go to bed, and arise to go to work again. Then they go to the bar, and then they go home to fuss at their wives again. They do this over and over again, and they call me and cry, "Pastor, you deal with a lot of people. Something is wrong with me. Why do I live this kind of existence?"

The answer is easy. This kind of person has left God out. No one has ever read and obeyed the Bible and gone wrong. It has never happened. God will never move you off course.

How many of you are under the oak tree of disobedience? There are some of you who are loose in your dating life. Or perhaps you need to join a church, but you are floundering from one thing to another. I want you to realize you are living under the oak tree of disobedience. Some of you should be sharing with God more of your finances, but you are not. You are living under the oak tree of disobedience. God promises that for every disobedience, there is retribution.

THE JUNIPER TREE

There is also the juniper tree of despair. In 1 Kings 19, beginning with verse 4, there is the text, "But he himself went a day's journey into the wilderness, and came and sat down

opened her eyes to full measure. She raised herself up on her elbows, and as her silver head lifted from the pillow, she began to sing, "I heard an old, old story, how a Savior came from glory." She got to the chorus, "O Victory in Jesus, my Savior forever. He sought me and bought me with His redeeming Blood." She then fell back on the pillow and went on to claim the victory.

Someone asked, "Gene, isn't it a shame your mother didn't get to finish the song?" He replied, "Oh, but she did. She and Daddy made it a duet in glory."

We have a Savior worth serving. There is, indeed, Victory in Jesus!

A well-known preacher at the 1980 Southern Baptist Convention challenged Christians in his eloquent and powerful way to "preach Jesus—the 'Master of the Mighty; Christ of the Conquerors; Head of the Heroes; Leader of the Legislators; Overseer of the Overcomers; Governor of the Governors; Prince of the Princes, King of Kings and Lord of Lords.' "

We have a Savior worth serving.

A CHURCH WORTH REVIVING

Second, we have a church worth serving. It really doesn't matter whether a church has a carpeted aisle or vinyl tile. It is not essential to know whether a pastor has a Th.D. or never had the opportunity for training. It's not important whether a church meets in a concrete-block building or a chapel of chiseled stones, or whether it sings a Bach anthem or a Gaither gospel, or even whether it has a pipe organ or a Hammond miniature. Those are not the ultimate issues.

What does matter is that within the church walls the Holy Spirit of God does his work, and sinners are converted and God's name is glorified. A revived church is a caring and sharing church.

Churches shouldn't be a cloistered crowd creating cultural calisthenics, but a lighthouse where men in the darkness can be saved; a rock for those sinking in life's despair; a hope for

under a juniper tree: and he requested for himself that he might die; and said, It is enough; now, O Lord, take away my life; for I am not better than my fathers."

Here was a prophet sitting under a juniper tree. He was moaning, "Poor me. God, just kill me." Have you ever been under the juniper tree of despair? That feeling came to a prophet of God because the prophet had been so despairing. Why had he been so despairing? Because he hadn't had a consistent daily walk with the Lord. That can happen to a music director, to a singing group, to a celebrity, or to a pastor. We can become so busy doing religious things that we don't have time for God.

Elijah had been ministering and pouring his life into the lives of others, but he was so drained that he had no spiritual resources for his own life.

Have you ever been under the juniper tree of despair? The answer is the same as it is for anyone else. Quit looking at your circumstances and look at God. A pessimist finds a problem in every opportunity, but an optimist finds opportunity in every problem.

I like the story of a general who said to a private, "We are surrounded by the enemy. Don't let one of them escape." Do you have that kind of encouragement? I hope you do. Don't despair, for God is the answer.

THE MULBERRY TREE

Consider the mulberry tree of awareness. In 2 Samuel 5 we can see where God is talking about another tree. Begin with verse 24, "And let it be, when thou hearest the sound of a going in the tops of the mulberry trees, that then thou shalt bestir thyself: for then shall the Lord go out before thee, to smite the host of the Philistines."

He advised, "David, don't you make a move until you get word from me. Then when you hear the sound in the mulberry trees . . . . " David and his armies were resting, and all

of a sudden there was a noise in the tree tops. David declared, "That's the sign God gave me. That's the sound of the mulberry tree." I am referring to the mulberry trees of awareness. David knew the awareness of the presence of God when he heard it. Many will come to the mulberry tree of awareness. Where has your mulberry tree of awareness been?

For some, they are on the hospital bed, pleading, "Oh God, if only that would not be malignant. God, if it will just be benign, I will serve you." Then the report comes back from the lab that everything is all right. The grateful person comes to church for three or four weeks, then returns to the pool of mediocrity once again because he didn't really mean it. Maybe God gave you a mulberry tree of awareness through a time of sickness.

For some of you, your mulberry tree is when you have come to a church and there has been a small casket. I have had people lament to me, "Preacher, the death of my child has reminded me of how I need to be loyal to God." And they are for awhile.

Listen, we had better be aware of the signs of God in the leaves of the mulberry tree because God can rustle that tree again. God can send that earthquake or that tornado and that wind of psychotic power into our lives.

For some of you the mulberry tree can be a great revival meeting. We have had many people become aware during our crusades. I know a dope addict who went cold turkey. I know an alcoholic that is now sober. He looked at me recently and affirmed, "Preacher, I don't even have any temptation that I will ever take a drink again. I don't have any fear of it. God has made me aware of what I ought to be."

Listen, my dear friend, I hear the sound of God rustling through the mulberry trees, saying to some, "Today is the day of salvation. Now is the accepted time." Listen, don't you hear that still small voice? God is saying, "I am rustling the leaves for you. Come and know me." Hear the sound that makes

you aware—the sound of the blessed music, the sound of your preacher, the sound of God stirring the mulberry trees that you might hear his voice.

THE FELLOWSHIP TREE

There is another tree. There is the tree of fellowship. I want you to see this tree. It is in Genesis 18.

> And the Lord appeared unto him in the plains of Mamre: and he sat in the tent door in the heat of the day; And he lift up his eyes and looked, and, lo, three men stood by him: and when he saw them, he ran to meet them from the tent door, and bowed himself toward the ground. And said, My Lord, if now I have found favour in thy sight, pass not away, I pray thee, from thy servant: Let a little water, I pray you, be fetched, and wash your feet, and rest yourselves under the tree.

These people came together and had love, joy, and fellowship. Don't you love fellowship? God's family reunion ought to include all the people of God. This is our family. This is our church family, our Christian family.

The Bible in this passage told how they fellowshipped and broke bread together. Thank God for the fellowship of the church. If you tell me you have been born again, but you are not active and faithful in a New Testament church, I doubt with all my heart that you have ever truly been born again. I am not judging you. I am expecting proof. I am a "fruit inspector."

Jesus declared that by their fruits shall you know them. John stated that you will know you have passed from death unto life if you love the brethren. A person who doesn't want to go to church is going to be miserable in heaven because it will be fellowship for eternity. If good preaching makes you nervous, you are going to be miserable in the presence of

God. God is not going to force heaven upon you. If you don't enjoy church, you can't enjoy heaven. Christ died for the church. He established the church, and at the rapture, he's coming back for the church to receive us unto himself. I love fellowshipping. The tree of fellowship is a wonderful tree.

THE WILLOW TREE

Then, think of the willow tree of lost joy. Psalm 137 poignantly expresses it, "By the rivers of Babylon, there we sat down, yea, we wept, when we remembered Zion. We hanged our harps upon the willows in the midst thereof."

David was talking about Israel. He was talking about the day they hung their harps in the willow trees and gave up. They lost their joy. They put their harps up. It's like a preacher putting his Bible on the shelf and saying, "I don't need it anymore."

Have you ever hung your harp upon the willow tree? Have you ever said you were not going to sing anymore or play anymore or be happy anymore. Sin causes that kind of lost joy. When someone is rude to me, I no longer become offended because I know something is wrong in their life. Do you have sin in your life? Sin causes a loss of joy.

The Bible teaches that the guilty flees when no man pursues. How true that is! Sin causes a person to lose his joy for Christ. If your sins don't make you lose your joy, you are lost. A Christian cannot sin and enjoy it. God fixes you when you are saved so you will never be able to sin again and "be comfortable with it."

Have you ever hung the harp on the willow tree and said, "God, I don't have any joy in my salvation"? What a horrible thought.

THE LIFE TREE

The last tree I want us to consider is the tree of life. Revelation 22:2: "In the midst of the street of it, and on either side of

the river, was there the tree of life, which bare twelve manner of fruits, and yielded her fruit every month: and the leaves of the tree were for the healing of the nations."

That is one tree I have never seen, but I am going to see it one day. Praise God, I am going to see it. Aren't you glad Jesus is alive. Jesus Christ is not only well and alive in heaven, but he is also alive here.

I know there is a tree of life. What is the root of that tree? Conversion to Jesus Christ. The trunk of that tree is consistent living. The branches of that tree are the witnesses of the saints. The fruit of that tree is souls being saved.

Are you part of the tree of life? Is your name written in the Lamb's book of life? Are you resting under the shade of God's protection? If you are under the tree of life, that's the place from which you can never be moved. One can never be moved, and that tree cannot be cut out from under you.

Be a part of the tree of life, for there is joy, eternal salvation, and security forever.

2
The Worth of the Work

Presidential Address, SBC
June 9, 1981
Los Angeles, California

The first "Bold Mission Thrust" is recorded in Acts 4. "Now when they saw the *boldness* of Peter and John . . . . " In other words, their boldness was obvious and that boldness came from the fact that they believed the work of Christ was worth whatever the price. They said, "For we cannot but speak the things which we have seen and heard."

Notice that their bold mission was empowered by the Holy Spirit which resulted in a new togetherness. "And when they had prayed, the place was shaken where they were assembled together; and they were all filled with the Holy Ghost, and they spake the Word of God with boldness. And the multitude of them that believed were of one heart and one soul" (Acts 4:31-32).

In this day of compromise and vacillation, an appropriate theme for us is "Our Bold Response Now!" *Now* is the day for us to speak the claims of Christ and respond to the needs of a hungry, lonely, needy, waiting world.

While president of the Southern Baptist Convention, it was my privilege to travel across this great land, as well as abroad, seeing Christians in many and varied types of work.

Many of them told of the challenges of the work, yet never with a regret or complaint. In almost every place, I asked the missionaries one consistent question: "Do you think it's worth it?"

In one of our pioneer mission areas, a precious pastor's wife had just related how long it had been since she had a new dress. She was asked if it was worth it. She answered, "I've never doubted that a moment." A vocational evangelist, who preaches about forty-three weeks a year and misses many events in the life of his family, was asked the same question. He said, "It's God's will. Sure, it's worth it." A denominational official in Nashville, Tennessee, answered the same way, as did a seminary professor.

An African missionary was walking back out of the deep Kenyan bush, after seeing nine people invite Jesus into their hearts at a little settlement. This missionary, perspiring in that hot East African sun, said, "I wouldn't do anything else."

The bold response from every Christian should be that the work and opportunity God has given is a worthy work.

We respond boldly to a waiting world because we have five great things to share.

A SAVIOR WORTH SERVING

First, we have a savior worth serving. The Word is a testimony to his uniqueness and greatness. "All things were made by Him; and without Him was not anything made that was made" (John 1:3). "For by him were all things created, that are in heaven, and that are in earth, visible and invisible, whether they be thrones, or dominions, or principalities, or powers. All things were created by him, and for him" (Col. 1:16).

Paul said in Philippians that Jesus who, being in the form of God, thought it not robbery to be equal with God and took upon himself the form of a servant, made himself of no reputation and "became obedient unto death, even the death of

THE WORTH OF THE WORK

the cross." The passage continues, "At the name of Jesus every knee shall bow . . . and every tongue shall confess that Jesus Christ is Lord to the glory of God the Father. For in him dwelleth all the fullness of the Godhead bodily" (Col. 2:9).

Jesus Christ is not one of the prophets who came to earth to show a "part of the personality of Deity," as some say. He, in the flesh, was God incarnate. All man, as if No God. All God, as if no man. Someone observed, "When he was born, He was older than his mother and the same age as his father. He was the heavenly son of an earthly mother and an earthly son of a Heavenly Father."

None has ever been even similar to Jesus Christ, the only begotten Son of God.

The song writer said it beautifully, "Jesus, the very thought of Thee with sweetness fills my breast, but sweeter far thy face to see and in Thy presence rest."

Christians are not proclaimers of some theoretical, religious, or philosophical meanderings from the dusty libraries of antiquity—but ambassadors of One in whom only is salvation—the Lord Jesus Christ. The world's greatest need is not a teacher, because the problem is not ignorance—it is not a patriot because the problem is not nationalism, not a philanthropist because the problem is not poverty. But the world *does* need a Savior, because the problem is sin.

E. M. Bartlett wrote many songs that Christians love to sing. One of the songs he wrote is "Victory in Jesus." After he wrote that song he passed away.

Sometime after that his wife lay in a comatose state in a hospital. She had not spoken or moved a muscle for several days. One day their son came into her hospital room, put his hand under the oxygen tent on the aged arm of the dear lady whose husband had written so many of the old gospel songs. The son said, "Mother, it's Gene. Will you talk with me?" That sweet lady raised her hands to indicate she wanted the oxygen tent raised. The son pulled it back over her head, and she

THE WORTH OF THE WORK

those who face a dead-end street. Somewhere in our world a wife needs a husband made new by Christ; a little girl needs a new daddy; a young boy needs a loving mother. A Church ablaze with Great Commission compassion can bring that about through the power of Christ.

Years ago in England lived a fine preacher named John Holden. One late afternoon in the village where he lived, everyone began to run to the seashore to man rowboats to go out into the sea where a vessel had capsized. Several small boats went out to bring to shore those who had been thrown into the icy waters.

As the last rowboat came in, John Holden, standing on shore, called out to the boat, "Did you get the last one?" The reply came from the little boat, "I think there's one more, but I can't find him."

John Holden began immediately to prepare to go out in his own small boat. His mother grabbed him and said, "Oh, Son, it's so dark and foggy—don't go out there. You may never come back." John Holden said, "Mother, I love you, but I've got to go out there."

After what seemed to be an interminable time, John Holden's little rowboat could be seen through the night and fog. Someone on shore shouted out, "Did you get him? Was there one more out there? Did you get him?" "Yes, I got him and tell my mother, it's my brother."

The revived church must go out on life's sea and bring men and women and boys and girls to the shore. Only a revived church can do the job. One of the greatest songs still is, "We have heard the joyful sound, Jesus Saves—Jesus Saves. Shout salvation full and free, Jesus Saves—Jesus Saves."

A DENOMINATION WORTH SUPPORTING

Third, we have a denomination worth supporting. The Southern Baptist Convention is the greatest force ever put together for winning this world to Christ. God must be sought in prayer to keep blessing it, enriching it, strengthening it, and

binding it together in love and harmony.

The annual income of the eight leading electronic evangelists are spread over a range of from 60 million dollars down to 11 million dollars, for a grand total of 293 million dollars. With no thought of disparaging the work of these good men of God, it has been pointed out that their budgets supported two churches, five schools, one hospital, TV ministries and some special and periodic mission work.

Let's contrast that with the work of the Southern Baptist Convention. In a recent year the mission income totaled 316 million. But these mission funds supported 6,000 full-time missionaries in more than ninety countries, six seminaries (10,000 students), 67 colleges, schools, and Bible institutions, 1,100 Baptist student directors, thirty-two radio and TV programs each week, and leadership materials for 35,255 Southern Baptist congregations which have averaged 1,000 baptisms per day for the past twenty-five years!

The Bold Mission Thrust of the Southern Baptist Convention is right on target because Southern Baptists have the capacity to bring Jesus to a lost and dying world. We could actually confront our world with the glorious Gospel of Jesus Christ by the year 2000 if we unite in a common cause.

A BIBLE WORTH BELIEVING

Fourth, we have a Bible worth believing. It's imperative that we believe the Bible to be totally the Word of God. We must believe the Bible is the infallible Word of God. Southern Baptists adopted as a Statement of Faith in 1963 its position on the Bible. It says, "The Holy Bible was written by men divinely inspired and is the record of God's revelation of Himself to man. It is a perfect treasure of divine instruction. It has God for its author, salvation for its end, and truth, without any mixture of error, for its matter." All of the above is important to believe.

If the Bible is the Word of God at all, it is the perfect Word of God, because God will not give a word of flaws and mis-

takes. A prominent pastor of one of our leading churches is exactly right when he says, "If the Bible is truthful, it must be truthful in all parts. Because truth and error are mutually exclusive. And if it's not true in all parts, who is to determine which part is truth and which part is error?"

Christians must never get bogged down in anything that keeps us from missions and evangelism, but no soldier wants to go into battle with a defective weapon. Believers can have confidence in the Word of God for we do have a Bible worth believing—sixty-six books, 1,189 chapters and 31,175 verses, all the true, inspired Word of God without any mixture of error.

A FUTURE WORTH LIVING

The fifth truth to remember is that we have a future worth living. Christians have a magnificent future in fulfilling the Great Commission of our Lord Jesus Christ. Every Bible-believing church has a future worth living because "the gates of hell shall not prevail against it." Each child of God has a great future because for one to put faith in Jesus Christ, he can rest assured that what Jesus said is true: "In my Father's house are many mansions, if it were not so I would have told you. I go to prepare a place for you . . . that where I am there you may be also" (John 14:2-3).

Jesus is coming again, too. Sometime ago, I stood at the graves of my parents. My mother had been in the hospital for routine surgery, but died there at forty-one years of age. My father was examining the foundation of a new auditorium he had led his church to build when a piece of reinforcement wire struck him in the eye. He fell dead at the age of fifty-five. They are buried side by side.

As I stood there, I remembered the times when Mom and Dad drove down the road, and Dad would put his right hand down on the seat. Mother would take her left hand and put it on his and down the road we would go. She would always do that—put her hand on his.

I thought of that coming day when Jesus shall appear. The graves will open, and I believe Dad will come out of one and Mom out of the other. I can imagine that Dad will reach out his hand and Mom will take his and, hand in hand, they shall rise and forever be with the Lord. There is a great, grand, and glorious future for everyone in Jesus Christ.

God is on his throne and challenges us to love one another because there is a world with a need to which we must minister.

May I share a poem that enriches and challenges everytime I recall it? Perhaps it can be a motto for the days ahead. The author is unknown, but it says:

> The world's great heart is aching,
>   Aching fiercely in the night
> And God alone can hear it—
>   And God alone give light.
>
> The men to bear the message
>   And speak the living Word
> Are you and I, my brother,
>   And the missions who have heard.
>
> We grovel among trifles
>   And our spirits fret and toss
> While above us burns the vision
>   Of Christ upon The Cross.
>
> And the Blood of Christ is streaming
>   From His pierced hands and side.
> And the lips of Christ are saying
>   Tell the lost that I have died.
>
> No power of man shall thwart us
>   No strongholds shall dismay
> When God commands obedience
>   And love has led the way.

3
Five Fruitful Failures

Galatians 6:7-8 reminds us, "Be not deceived; God is not mocked: for whatsoever a man soweth, that shall he also reap. For he that soweth to his flesh shall of the flesh reap corruption; but he that soweth to the Spirit shall of the Spirit reap life everlasting."

It is not only true that success breeds success, but it is true that failure breeds failure. Sometimes the most fruitful things in all of the world are failure and sin. Sin has its way of multiplying and snowballing in its effect to an extent that sin which is begun is hardly recognized when it is through because of how it seams together.

The Old Testament prophets said that the fathers had eaten sour grapes and the children's teeth were set on edge. Sin has a way of doing that. Just like a pebble thrown into the lake, the ripples seems to keep going out. Man cannot hope to sow briars and one day harvest corn. It won't happen. "For whatsoever a man soweth, that shall he also reap." When a person sows sinful failures, they are going to continue and there is going to be unbelievable tragedy when a person has forgotten God's principle that whatever he plants, he will one day harvest. Whatever sin, whether it be sin of commission or sin of omission, he will reap.

We will see in the Scriptures where men who failed bore the bitter fruits of their sinful decadence and failures.

TO DISOBEY IS TO BE DESTROYED

Our first reference is in Daniel 5:1-4:

> Belshazzar the king made a great feast to a thousand of his lords, and drank wine before the thousand. Belshazzar, whiles he tasted the wine, commanded to bring the golden and silver vessels which his father Nebuchadnezzar had taken out of the temple which was in Jerusalem; that the king, and his princes, his wives, and his concubines, might drink therein. Then they brought the golden vessels that were taken out of the temple of the house of God which was at Jerusalem; and the king, and his princes, his wives, and his concubines, drank in them. They drank wine, and praised the gods of gold, and of silver, of brass, of iron, of wood, and of stone.

Here was a man who had been told by God to clean up his act. He had been told by God to live righteously, and yet all of the precepts and principles of the statutes of God were totally ignored. Belshazzar, who was the grandson of Nebuchadnezzar, decided that he would have a feast. He was only the head of the *city* of Babylon. He was not the head of the empire of Babylon, but he was head of the city of Babylon.

He decided he would have a feast. It didn't matter what God wanted him to do. It really didn't matter about the standards of the world or the qualifications which God had put upon him. He just didn't care. So he had a drunken blast with the dancing girls in their flimsy garments, the Oriental birds singing, and the various fountains sparkling.

The night air was blowing in, bringing cooling to all the lords and guests who were there. Belshazzar then decided that he would go one step further. He called for all of the golden vessels (which we would call the Lord's Supper glasses) from

FIVE FRUITFUL FAILURES

the Temple of God and took an intoxicating beverage and began to pour it into the vessels that had been sanctified to God. Then he began to drink from them. They, in their drunken orgy of pleasure, began to watch the dancing girls. Belshazzar hadn't a care in the world about what God had said.

Archaeologists have discovered while digging up the city of Babylon that there were rooms which would hold a thousand people seated at banquet tables. They have also discovered that the walls were 350 feet high and eighty-seven feet thick. They also discovered that the gate of Babylon was of solid, unblemished brass. Throughout Babylon meandering diagonally was the Euphrates River which was a further protection and fortress for the security of the king resting on his throne inside. Here was the man who proclaimed, "I don't care what God says. I don't care what seems to be going on. I don't care that these vessels were dedicated to God. I am going to do what I want to do."

Furthermore, he began to drink (make a toast) to the gods of gold, silver, and brass. If America can't follow God, it doesn't change its life—it changes its gods. Belshazzar couldn't do what he wanted to do by serving the God he disobeyed. So, he made himself a new god. Then he celebrated and built, in an idolatrous act, unto the god that he could serve—the god of gold, silver, and brass. He was defaming and disobedient.

The messenger came to him and reported, "Belshazzar, Darius is outside." Darius was king of the Medes who later joined up with the kings of the Persians. Belshazzar didn't blink an eye. He was protected by the walls of his great city and the Euphrates River. He was the king. He was only thirty-five years old and sitting upon the throne of authority. This message didn't bother him. He had more girls dance and more rebellion against God. But all of a sudden, they looked up and there was handwriting on the walls. The archaeologists have discovered that those walls had a chalky substance on them.

They could write on the wall with a finger like you can write on your window when it is covered with dampness during the winter.

He looked over and saw the words, "Mene, Mene, Tekel, Upharsin." He called all of his "scholars" together and asked them what it meant. His legs began to knock together. Finally the prophet Daniel came and explained, "God has taken his weights and put you on the other side of the scale. You have come out lacking."

Now Belshazzar the king who had been disobedient was being rushed by the armies of the Medes. They took their swords and thrust them into the hearts of that king and those men and women. Finally, the blood of those royal people suddenly mixed with the wine as it trickled down the marble steps of the palace. Belshazzar was now dead. Failure is fruitful. "Whatsoever a man soweth, that shall he also reap." Belshazzar, who had turned his back on God and taken that which was holy to defame it, was now being held accountable before Almighty God. The Bible teaches that your body is the Temple of the Holy Spirit. It is the chosen vessel of God. When you drink it up, smoke it up, drug it up, God is not at all pleased. Our bodies are the Temples of the Holy Spirit. Belshazzar took that which was holy, poured wine into it, and defamed it.

I wonder how much we are defaming the holy things of God. We get so nervous and uptight, and we blame it on our schedules. I have discovered there is enough time in every day to do everything God wants us to do with a sweet spirit. If you don't do something you should do, don't blame it on God. When a man begins to defame his body by his attitude, or his habits, pretty soon he begins to disobey the Scriptures, and destruction inevitably comes.

I visited a 46-year-old man some time ago in the hospital. He was dying of cancer. Since that visit, I have preached his

FIVE FRUITFUL FAILURES 33

funeral. When I visited him in the hospital, he reached over with a trembling hand and picked up a package of cigarettes. He then brought it to his lips. His lungs were eaten out by more than twenty years of smoking. He looked at that cigarette, then at a picture of his family on the vanity table, then at me and sadly commented, "Preacher, it's not worth it, is it?" I replied, "No, sir, it is not."

My friend, if you are disobedient to God in the terms of your soul, you are going to destroy your soul. If you are disobedient to God in terms of your body, you will destroy your body. If you are disobedient to God in terms of your mind, you are going to destroy your mind. For when a person sows disobedience, he inevitably reaps destruction.

So many churches have allowed this to happen. They have worshiped form, so they are being destroyed by formality. They have worshiped culture, so they are being destroyed by cold, meaningless worship. Some men have worshiped money, and they have been destroyed by greed. For when a man sows disobedience, he reaps destruction. What a fruitful failure disobedience is.

TO BE LOOSE IS TO BE LONELY

Second, when a person sows looseness, he reaps loneliness. We refer to 1 Samuel 15:21-26:

> But the people took of the spoil, sheep and oxen, the chief of the things which should have been utterly destroyed, to sacrifice unto the Lord thy God in Gilgal. And Samuel said, Hath the Lord as great delight in burnt offerings and sacrifices, as in obeying the voice of the Lord? Behold, to obey is better than sacrifice, and to hearken than the fat of rams. For rebellion is as the sin of witchcraft, and stubbornness is as iniquity and idolatry. Because thou hast rejected the word of the Lord, he hath also re-

jected thee from being king. And Saul said unto Samuel, I have sinned: for I have transgressed the commandment of the Lord, and thy words: because I feared the people, and obeyed their voice. Now therefore, I pray thee, pardon my sin, and turn again with me, that I may worship the Lord. And Samuel said unto Saul, I will not return with thee: for thou hast rejected the word of the Lord, and the Lord hath rejected thee from being king over Israel.

Saul was different from Belshazzar. Saul was supposed to know God; Belshazzar really didn't. Belshazzar was the out-and-out disobedient person who shakes his fist in the face of God and says, "God, I don't care what you say. Forget it! I don't care about you or your Bible or your church! I don't care about your preachers! God, just forget it." That kind of person is a disobedient person to God.

But on the other hand, Saul wasn't that disobedient in his own mind. He simply had to edit everything God said. His problem was looseness. When one sows looseness, he reaps loneliness.

Saul had become loose—fast and free—with God's commands. No longer was God going to recognize him as king. This man's finest friend was Samuel, the prophet of God. But Samuel said, "Saul, God may have forgiven you, but I will no longer be your friend. I will no longer walk with you."

It is a lonely thing to sin. It is a lonely thing to become loose. Many want to change God's Word. Samuel knew what Saul was doing. God had told him, "Saul, I want you to go in and when you take the Amalekites, I want you to kill every one of them. I want you to take King Agag and he also is to be killed." When Samuel approached Saul, and said, "Saul, is it true that you spared the animals and brought them back to make money off them?" Saul protested, "Oh, no, I didn't do that." All of a sudden, the sound of the animals was heard.

FIVE FRUITFUL FAILURES *35*

Samuel asked what the sound was, but Saul insisted that he knew nothing.

"Be sure your sin will find you out." Here was a man who said, "God really didn't mean it. I know he said to kill them all and not to save any of the spoil, but God didn't really mean it."

I want you to understand, without any shadow of a doubt, that everything God has ever said, he means! It is not our place or our right to go through the Bible and say, "Yes, I know what it says, but God didn't really mean it." When we begin to sow looseness, or become careless with the things of God, take some of the Bible in, and leave some of the Bible out, you will be inevitably lonely. Soon you will lose the trust of God. You will lose the confidence of the preachers. You will lose the friendship of those who want spiritual fellowship with you. You might even lose your family.

Brokenhearted people have lamented to me, "Preacher, when I began to get away from the things of God, I lost my spouse, children, and everything that was important to me. Why?" Because when a man sows looseness, he reaps loneliness.

One horrible fact about looseness with your morals and with the Scriptures is that it leads to loneliness. I have had people remark, "Well, Preacher, what is right for you, may be wrong for me. We all have our different standards." Sin is not relative. If it is wrong for you, it is wrong for me. Your conscience is not God. Your evaluation of sin is not God. God is God. Whatever God has taught is wrong, is wrong. Whatever God teaches is right, is right. God doesn't want you to be like Saul and say, "Yes, I know what God says, but . . . . " There is liberalism and conservatism. There is truth and no truth. There is adherence to the Scriptures and disobedience. There is looseness which eventually brings loneliness. When a man sows looseness in his marriage, business, or life, he soon knows what it is to be lonely.

TO SIN IS TO SUFFER

Third, not only when a person sows disobedience will he reap destruction; not only when he sows looseness will he reap loneliness; but also notice that when he sows sin, he will reap suffering. That's another fruitful failure. Reference is now made to Judges 16:20-21:

> And she said, The Philistines be upon thee, Samson. And he awoke out of his sleep, and said, I will go out as at other times before, and shake myself. And he wist not that the Lord was departed from him. But the Philistines took him, and put out his eyes, and brought him down to Gaza, and bound him with fetters of brass; and he did grind in the prison house.

Here was a strong and mighty man with vision and spiritual integrity. But, all of a sudden, he became a man who was weak, blind, and without the presence of the Lord in his life. He was totally unaware that God's presence and power had left him. And mind you, it was in the dispensation when the Spirit of God would come upon a person, empower him, leave him, and then return when special power was needed. How can we say those things about the same man? Here was a seemingly strong man. Here was a weak man. Here was a man with God. Here was a man without God. Here was a moral man. Here was an immoral man. Here was a man who was as pure as a Nazarite. Here was a man who was as impure as the most lost man who had ever lived.

In two hours of his life, sin entered in. When a person sows sin, he reaps suffering. Samson was the strong and mighty man of God. And yet, his eyes had been blinded and he was grinding at the mill. This is one of the saddest spectacles I can imagine. Poor Samson. God had told him to leave that trashy harlot alone, but he didn't do it. He had previously fallen into

trouble with another woman and continued to sow sin. Finally, there was suffering.

Listen, before it is too late, whatever advice we can give to others, we need to take it ourselves. Samson knew what was wrong for everyone. He was an effective man. He could set the Philistines on fire, but he couldn't control the fire of lust that was burning in his own heart. He could kill a lion, but he couldn't slay the passions that ate up his soul. He could take those bonds that were placed around him and burst them, but he could not break the shackles of sin wrapped around his own immoral tendencies.

There are some fathers who know how to lecture their children to stay off dope, but Daddy is not such a hot Christian himself because he can't leave alcohol alone. He who sows sin will reap suffering. Turn before it is too late.

TO BE JEALOUS IS TO BE JUDGED

When a man sows jealousy, he reaps judgment. That's the fourth fruitful failure. Genesis 4:11:

> And now art thou cursed from the earth, which hath opened her mouth to receive thy brother's blood from thy hand.

God said he wanted a worthy sacrifice. Abel put the bullock on the altar as he was supposed to do. Cain put the fruits and vegetables he had raised by the works of his own hands on the altar, and God did nothing about it. When Abel put the offering of the slain lamb upon the altar, the fire of God came and consumed that offering, but when Cain put his fruits and vegetables on the altar, it remained on the altar. God didn't receive it. God didn't want it. Cain said, "Look at all *I* have done." Don't you know the Bible teaches that Cain's real problem was not a jealousy against Abel, but really a jealousy against *God's* way?

There are still people like that. There are people who say,

"I don't care what you people believe. I still believe it is by a man's works that he gets to heaven."

Ephesians 2:8-9 declares, "For by grace are ye saved through faith; and that not of yourselves: it is the gift of God: Not of works, lest any man should boast."

There are people who claim, "We don't believe in the judgment of God." John 3:36 says, "He that believeth on the Son hath everlasting life: and he that believeth not the Son shall not see life; but the wrath of God abideth on him." Others argue, "I just don't believe that people who are lost die and go to hell." Revelation 21:8 says, "But the fearful, and unbelieving, and the abominable, and murderers, and whoremongers, and sorcerers, and idolaters, and all liars, shall have their part in the lake which burneth with fire and brimstone: which is the second death."

A person who becomes jealous of the ways of God is one who inevitably finds that the judgments of God are sure. Some can argue all day long with what the Bible teaches, but someday they are going to discover that they will be standing before the unalterable judgment of God and they will hear, "Depart from me. I never knew you."

First John 3:12 indicates that it was Cain's attitude against God and Cain's own self-righteousness that sent him away from God. Jesus stated in Luke that the Pharisees were guilty of killing Jesus and guilty of Cain's sin. The sin of Cain is the same as the sin of the Pharisees. The Pharisees thought that if they were religious and "prayed" ornate prayers, everything would be all right. Do you know what the "religious" men's problems are? They are akin to what Paul said about religionists. They were stumbling over the simplicity of the cross of Christ.

Since Jesus shed his blood on Calvary's cross, that blood can wash one clean of his sins. It can set one free and give one the promise of eternal life. A person can argue with that or debate it or be jealous. But it remains true. Whatever one's

reaction is, it does not alter the truth of God.

In Matthew 6:11, Jesus said, "Give us this day our daily bread." Notice how a lawyer rewrote this verse, "We respectfully petition, request, and entreat that due and adequate provision be made this day and the day hereinafter subscribed for the satisfying of these petitioners' nutritional requirements and for the organizing of such methods of allocation and distribution as may be deemed necessary and proper to assure the reception by and for said petitioners of such quantities of baked cereal products as shall in the judgment of the aforesaid petitioners constitute a sufficient supply thereof." However, Jesus simply said, "Give us this day our daily bread."

The Bible declares that without the shedding of blood, there is no remission of sin. "For whosoever shall call upon the name of the Lord shall be saved" (Rom. 10:13). We can complicate it with all our religious jargon, but there is no other way to know Christ other than through accepting what he did upon the cross for our salvation. No amount of religion will ever accomplish that.

One lady said to me, "You narrow-minded Baptists think one religion is better than another." I said, "No, ma'am. All religions are just as good as another." To which she replied, "Oh, you must be fairer than most Baptists." I said, "No, ma'am. I believe that all religions are as good as another. In fact, I believe all religions are as bad as another. In fact, all religions will send you to hell." Mere religion is the greatest curse that ever came to mankind. Religion will send you to hell, but Jesus will give you eternal life.

TO BE HARD BRINGS HEARTACHE

The fifth fruitful failure is this: When a man sows hardness, he reaps heartache. In Exodus 4:21-23, we read:

> And the Lord said unto Moses, When thou goest to return into Egypt, see that thou do all those won-

ders before Pharaoh, which I have put in thine hand: but I will harden his heart, that he shall not let the people go. And thou shalt say unto Pharaoh, Thus saith the Lord, Israel is my son, even my firstborn: And I say unto thee, Let my son go, that he may serve me: and if thou refuse to let him go, behold, I will slay thy son, even thy firstborn.

Chapter 5:2 says, "And Pharaoh said, Who is the Lord, that I should obey his voice to let Israel go? I know not the Lord, neither will I let Israel go."

What does it mean that God hardened the heart of Pharaoh? It does not mean that God caused his heart to be hard, but it means the very presence of God made Pharaoh's heart to be hardened because God was there. Had no one ever encountered Pharaoh or crossed him, he would have been fine. But the very existence of God made him angry, made his heart calloused and hardened.

While visiting the other day I went to a door, and when I mentioned God, the door slammed. The very mention of God at that home caused anger, reaction, and a hardened heart. If one were to go into a bar today and walk up to the counter and say, "Folks, let's all turn to John 3:16," he would certainly get a reaction.

The Bible means that Pharaoh would not obey God and would not listen to God, so he hardened his heart against God because he refused to go the way of God. It wasn't God who did it—it was Pharaoh's reaction to God.

The same sunshine that melts snow will harden clay. It all depends on what you are made of. There are some people who have heard the voice of God, and they have been suffering, and they have turned to God, and their lives have been transformed. But there are others who have heard his voice, and they have hardened their hearts, and it has brought heartache.

There are some to whom God says, "I want your talent," and they refuse. When they do, it brings them heartache. To some God has said, "I want you to teach." They have refused, and it has brought the heartache of young children going untaught. To some God has requested their marriage be revived, but they hardened their hearts so much toward God that they have ended up in the divorce courts.

When a person sows hardness, he reaps heartache. Here is a good word for you. Just as failure is fruitful, so it is that when a man lives for God, all the generations to come will be blessed. Throw a rock into the sea of life, and watch the ripples go; but make sure you want to harvest what you plant.

4
The Result of Revival

Revival is immanent in America. If that be true, there will be certain results coming from that kind of Holy Spirit visitation.

The story of the Prodigal Son in Luke 15 is not of a sinner "finding" the father, but of a sinner "coming back" to the father. It is the account of one who knew the home, parents, protection, and love of a family, but who ran away from it. He went in sin, but had a revival and came back. Now that's my conviction about it and its implications.

The purpose of Luke 15 was not merely to tell the story of the Prodigal Son but was shared by Jesus to counter criticism. He encountered the criticism of the Pharisees and the scribes who didn't like the fact that Jesus loved and cared for sinners. Luke 15 is no more than Jesus using the sheep, the coin, and the son to illustrate how God will save those who are away and those who are lost. The other side of the story was told, pointing to the fact that the Pharisees are like the older brother. In other words, the "star" of Luke 15 is the older brother. Jesus told Luke 15 in order to teach the Pharisees, "Look, I'm going to tell you who you are like. You are like the older brother."

Old filthy, dirty sinners still love Jesus. They just love to come to Jesus. But, of course, they can't get saved if they hear only theologians. People say, "Why don't you quote

more theologians?" Why quote number 4,000 when you can quote number one? Just preach the Bible.

All of the parables in Luke 15 were presented as Jesus gave a rebuttal to the criticism of the Pharisees. The coin was lost, but it was found. The sheep was lost, but it was found. The son was lost, but he was found. The older brother went away, and we do not know if he *ever* came back. Jesus said that the religious folks "won't get in." He was explaining to them that in this story there was a revival. Something is seriously wrong with those who don't rejoice in revival.

If a person doesn't love to see revival, he is either lost or horribly backslidden. Let's look at what happens when revival comes to town.

SIN IS SEEN AS SERIOUS

The Bible says that when that prodigal son was in the hog pen, he came to himself. No one has ever really thought seriously about Jesus and turned him down.

Jesus said in Luke 15:17, "And when he came to himself, he said to himself, I will arise and go to my father." When a person says "no" to Christ, it is because he is not person enough to think for himself. He is letting the devil say "no" for him. The Bible shows that when a person comes to himself—when he gets down to that gut level and when he truly gets rid of the superficial, the fog, and all of the resistance he has put on over the years—all of the other issues just don't matter. When a person really gets down to himself, Jesus said that person will inevitably come to God.

When the son came to himself, he affirmed, "I will arise and go to my father." What happened to him? He began to see that *his sin was serious*. Notice how he began to compare what he had now to what he used to have. Here he was eating hog slop—back home he could have had prime rib. The only thing over his head here was the sky. He could have had the roof of a loving father over his head back home. He began to

THE RESULT OF REVIVAL

talk to himself, *Man, am I stupid.*

When America comes to revival, we are not going to tolerate some things that we put up with today. The television screens will be cleaned up. The movies will be cleaned up. Broadway will be cleaned up. Hollywood will be cleaned up. Some churches will be cleaned up. Lives will be changed. The world that's in the hog pen today can't stay there if God comes into their hearts. America needs to see that its sin is serious.

One of the most horrible sins today is the sin of ingratitude. We are a grumbling and ungrateful people. We don't care about what God has given us. We selfishly hang onto our money, afraid that God knows we really realize the fact that all we have belongs to him.

One time a little Christian boy sat down at a table of some lost people. They had just started eating. The boy was shocked because his mother and daddy always had prayer. The boy started praying, and it intimidated the head of the house. The head of the house interrupted the boy as he was praying and said, "Son, does everyone at your house pray?" He answered, "No, sir, our pigs don't."

When America has Spirit-filled, Holy Ghost revival, there will be a new sense of what is sinful, wrong, and hateful. America will fall upon its knees and cry, "God, we are sorry for what we have been. We are sorry for the way we have lived. We are sorry for the way we have acted. We are sorry for our ingratitude." It is amazing that God gives us water, and some people take their boats out on Sunday and forget about God. We take the very blessings of God and turn them against that holy and righteous God.

Of course, we have different names for sin today. Prostitutes are now "party girls"—no longer whores. We don't have drunks—we have alcoholics. However, it doesn't actually matter what you call it—it is still sin. Man calls it an accident; God calls it an abomination. Man calls it a blunder; God calls it blindness. Man calls it a defect; God calls it a disease. Man

calls it a short chance; God calls it a choice. Man calls it fascination; God calls it fatality. Man calls it infirmity; God calls it iniquity. Man calls it liberty; God calls it lawlessness. Man says he made a mistake; God calls it madness. It doesn't matter how many different words you call it. When anything anyone in this world does is against the Holy Book, it is sin.

I think it was Charles Haddon Spurgeon who used the finest illustration of sin I have ever heard. "Can you imagine a person going to his baby's bed and finding a snake coiled in the crib and seeing that the serpent had already bitten the child and the child was dead? Now imagine that person taking that snake, after killing it, and getting it out of the baby bed, taking it to the taxidermist and having the snake stuffed and having little pearls placed in his eye sockets for eyes, and putting lipstick on the lips of the snake, and then having the snake arranged on velvet backing and framing it. Then, putting it in the foyer of their home so that all of their friends could see it. When those friends would look at it, the parents would say proudly, 'Oh, that's the wonderful serpent that killed our baby as one day he was innocently sleeping in his bed. That's the serpent, and we framed him so you can admire the snake.' "

Now, you know we certainly would not do that. But, when any man, woman, boy or girl becomes enthusiastic about their sin, they are displaying the very evil spirit that killed God's son.

We have churches all over America filled with people who are proud of their sins. If revival does come to America, sin will be seen as serious. As I have previously said, the world doesn't need a teacher because the problem is not ignorance. The world does not need a philanthropist because the problem is not poverty. The world does not need a guru because the problem is not "religion." The world does not need a nationalist because the problem is not politics. The world *does need* a Savior because the problem is sin. When America has revival, sin will be seen as serious.

I know a young man who over thirteen years ago was

crawling around on his garage apartment floor when he was about seven months old. His father was out with another woman in a drunken stupor. He came up the stairs of the apartment. The mother was warming the bottle. The father opened the door to the apartment, and he saw his young son crawling around, and the father was so full of sin and liquor that he kicked that little baby in the ribs. That seven-month-old infant rolled down the stairs of that garage apartment and hit near the driveway.

The mother turned off the stove, and that excuse for a father fell back on the bed and laughed. The mother put the baby in the car and rushed him to the hospital. The baby's life was saved, but the kick and the fall caused a curvature of the spine. That man today is over twenty years of age and may never be able to be married. He will never be able to be a father, nor have the joys of life that some of us know. He will never have one normal day of his life because of his father's hideous sin. When America gets serious about God, America will have to get serious about its sin.

THE FATHER WILL BE FOUND FAITHFUL

The man in the hog pen began to see that sin is wrong and serious. If revival comes to America, not only is sin going to be seen as serious, but the Father will be found faithful. That's the greatest story in Luke 15. The Father was found faithful.

Imagine the son thinking, *I've really blown it now. I can never go back home.* But every day the father came to that stone fence around the home place, put his foot up on the fence, and leaned on his elbow to look for his boy. One day as he came to the fence, he saw the silhouette of a figure coming in the distance. He noticed the gait of the walk was one that he remembered. The form began to take shape as that of the younger son. Finally, he saw that indeed it was his boy. He called to everyone, "Come, greet my boy!" and he ran out to meet him.

I talked to a lady some time ago in an Eastern state. She

said, "Are you really president of the Southern Baptist Convention?" I answered, "Yes, I really am." She said, "I want you to know, I'm not going to be a Southern Baptist." I replied, "All right, I have an idea you would like to tell me why." She said, "I certainly would. I want to go to a denomination that has a higher concept of God. It's this matter of 'getting saved, being born again, the blood, the cross.' I want a church of a more formal atmosphere where there is a moral sphere; a concept of a Holy God."

Isn't that wonderful? But so ignorant. When God wanted you to know what he was like, he said, "I am a Father who wants the prodigal to come home." The greatest concept one can have of God is to be an active and evangelistic church—a church where people believe. Our Father is wanting sinners to be saved. That's where people are getting out of the hog pen.

Wouldn't it be marvelous if in the Southern Baptist Convention next Sunday, the churches were filled with prostitutes and drug users and alcoholics, and when the invitation was given, God's Spirit would fall and people would get right with the Holy God? The highest concept of God is that he is a Father who wants sinners to be saved.

The Father is found faithful in his love. Aren't you glad God loves us? The lost, dirty sinner can shake his fist in the face of God and say, "God, I don't care anything about you. I hate you, God." My friend, if you did that, there would be one response from God. He would say, "But I love you." The world out there needs to know there is a God who is faithful in his love.

Not only is he faithful in his love, but he is faithful in his forgiveness. I notice that the earthly father never brought up the past of the Prodigal Son. He never said, "You dirty rat, where have you been?" The characteristic of God is forgiveness. You say, "Yes, but don't you think we ought to have quality Christians?" I used to think so until I met some. The church needs to be full of sinners—sinners saved by God's

THE RESULT OF REVIVAL 49

grace. None of you are beyond that. That father was just so glad to have his son home that he said, "Son, come on in. I'm so glad you're here."

In Oklahoma there was a country song about "Uncle Roy." The story of the song is about Uncle Roy going to church and reading the Bible. He read, "For God so loved . . . . " and he yelled, "Hallelujah, praise the Lord." Then he read another Scripture, "For by grace are ye saved through faith." He shouted, "Hallelujah." Then, his Bible was taken away from him. His behavior and shouting was destroying the austerity of the church. He picked up a hymn book and read, "Amazing grace, how sweet the sound that saved a wretch like me," and he shouted, "Hallelujah," and woke everyone up again. So the hymn book was taken away from him and finally, he simply shouted. They said, "Uncle Roy, we took the Bible away and we took the hymn book away. Why are you shouting?" He said, "Just to see the handiwork of God in this place." They said, "We'll fix you. We'll put you in the closet." So they put him in the closet with the brooms and mops and magazines, and everyone was just fine until, through the closed closet door, came, "Hallelujah, praise the Lord!" They opened the door and asked, "Uncle Roy, how could you shout in the closet?" He replied, "Oh, I was just reading the *National Geographic,* and it says that in one place the ocean is 34,000 feet deep and that is where Jesus put my sins!"

The Father is found faithful. He is faithful in his love. He is faithful in his forgiveness. He is faithful in his provisions. He is faithful in his consistency with us. There is never a moment when we have to be without the Lord.

Just a few years ago a pastor lost his 34-year-old wife in death. That man and his little daughter went back home after the funeral and that night the little girl said, "Daddy, could I sleep with you tonight? Daddy, I'm scared." It was a frightful thing for the father and the little girl to be without mother. He said, "Honey, that will be fine." The lights were out, and the

daddy was almost asleep when he felt something. It was the fingers of his little girl. He said, "Honey, is anything wrong?" She said, "No, sir, I just wanted to know if your face was towards me."

The world wants to know if God's face is towards them. Isn't it wonderful that we can say to a hurting, scared world, "The Father is faithful."

SINNERS WILL SEEK TO BE SAVED

There are two kinds of sinners: hell-bound sinners and heaven-bound sinners. Both need to be saved. One saved from hell and one saved from a hellish attitude. The Prodigal Son did not become prodigal by leaving home. He left home *because he was* a prodigal son. Already in his heart he had become one. A person does not become a thief by stealing; he steals because he is a thief. It is through that nature of sin that we will do these things. The Bible says that when revival comes, people will seek to be saved.

All across this country we are seeing "church members" being saved. The only people who become upset when lost church members are saved are other lost church members. Recently in Oklahoma two pastors' wives were saved. The organist of one of our large Baptist churches was saved. An 83-year-old deacon's wife was saved. Why? Because, when revival comes, all of those old crutches we have been leaning on, like baptism, church membership, and self-righteousness crumble around us, and we have to lean on something. If we look for Jesus to lean upon and he's not there, we know we need to be saved. When revival came to the heart of the prodigal, he wanted to come to the father.

In one of our Starlight Crusades sponsored by our church in Del City, we have had 1,365 people saved. The Holy Spirit of God was so prominent. I came in on a Sunday night and the telephone rang. A man asked, "Preacher, is it too late to be saved? My wife and I couldn't go to sleep tonight." I said,

THE RESULT OF REVIVAL

"We had a great service, didn't we?" He said, "Yes, sir, that service Thursday night was really something." I said, "Wait a minute. You were not in church tonight?" He said, "No, but since Thursday night we have not been able to sleep because the Holy Spirit's conviction has been so great." I said, "Do you have an extension phone?" He said, "No, you will have to help us be saved one by one." And I did. He was saved and then his wife was saved—on the telephone!

The Holy Spirit was there with such power, we would walk into the crusade and people would be saved before the service, during the service, and during the message. People were being witnessed to and won to Christ as the message was being preached. When revival comes, sinners know that God is near and awesome. In those who have spiritual needs, or a desire for spiritual maturity, there is an excitement and a joy.

My wife and I used to go by the nursery after the services and pick up our little baby. People would be coming out of our church after the baptismal service at 11 or 12 at night. They would be hugging each other, and I would ask my wife, "Honey, aren't you glad we are not liberals?" It's fun to see people being saved. I'd see those big men hugging their brothers because those brothers had been saved. Doctors would be hugging lawyers. One day a deaf member brought a blind lady to Christ. When revival comes, sinners seek the Lord. There is a spirit of expectancy. There is a happiness about folks being saved. There is a joy that cannot be known in any other experience of life. When God is near, something happens.

Several years ago I was coming out of the stadium after a Starlight service with my wife by my side, and this beautiful brunette came running up to us, almost shouting, "Preacher, it happened. It happened." She grabbed me, hugged me, and kissed me right on the face, all the while saying, "It happened, it happened." Then she ran off. I said, "I hope it happens again." I found out what had happened. Her father had been

saved that night. There is nothing like a service where people get saved. The same holds true for the service where people don't get saved. There is no comparison between the two. There's a joy and a thrill when people are born again.

HYPOCRITES WILL HARBOR HATEFULNESS

If you want to know who the hypocrites in your church are, just have revival. They will show up and let you know the music was too loud, or that the preacher hollers too much, or that the service ran too late. Notice the hypocrite in the story of Luke 15. Everyone was rejoicing because the Prodigal Son had come home. The fatted calf had been killed. There was excitement and joy, but there was one son with his bottom lip all "pooched" out. He couldn't have cared less. He was mad and upset. He didn't want anyone to be saved. He didn't want anyone to get right.

A family left the church service and the father said, "That was the worst sermon I ever heard." The little girl said, "Yes, and the piano player must never have had a lesson." The little boy finally looked at his daddy and said, "Yes, but it wasn't such a bad show for a nickel, was it?"

One preacher had a man in his church named Brother So-n-So who had a gripe or complaint at every business meeting. Finally, the preacher couldn't stand it anymore and said, "Brother So-n-So, would you please stand and lead us in a word of criticism?"

The Bible demonstrates that revival turns over the superficial topsoil of religious activity, exposing that attitude to the sunlight of God's wisdom. It then becomes obvious who is a hypocrite. He doesn't want to pay the price of revival. He doesn't want to stay long enough. When revival takes place, one cannot be time-conscious and be eternity-conscious. When revival comes, hypocrites will harbor hatefulness. Jeremiah 5 says, "They made their faces harder than a rock."

That older brother was mad because it was probably *his*

calf that was killed. The younger brother was out in the hog pen while that wonderful, outstanding young man who never left his father was home getting up at 4:30 in the AM feeding that calf, seeing about the mending of fences, tending to the crops. Therefore, that was *his* calf, *his* father, *his* table, *his* bedroom. This was *his* whole affair. Therefore, he wasn't about to be excited when they killed his calf.

Unless Baptists are willing to let some of their sacred calves die, we won't ever become excited about sinners being saved. For some, it's *their* auditorium. For others, it is *their* Sunday school class. We are holding on, but we must let it go. Some of us have sacred calves in our churches that we wouldn't kill if it meant the whole world being saved. It is our sacred calf, but if Jesus wants it dead for the Prodigal Son to come back home, we must be willing.

If you compared the two boys, the boy who stayed home would definitely be the better boy. But Jesus is teaching that the reason the older brother didn't get right, and the reason he went out and never got back in, is because he thought he was good for staying home and being a hard worker. He thought he was good for and being faithful to the father.

Many church members are going to die and go to hell because they are impressed with the money they give and how they sing or the time they give devotionals or how long they spend around the church building. But they, just like the older brother, have been faithful to the father. However, it will surface that they loved themselves more than being faithful to the Father. They don't love Jesus. The faithful son never got in.

There is a contempt in America for the invitation. My father used to preach and my grandfather used to preach, and from time to time great numbers of people would be saved. We would have invitations lasting thirty or forty minutes, and there would be crying and weeping.

We are going to lose power as a denomination if we get away from the fact that every sermon ought to end in a ver-

dict. Every sermon ought to end with dirty, rotten sinners being born again. The invitation ought to be the highlight.

What was wrong with the older brother? He hated the invitation. He thought, "Why don't we mail a check to the boy and leave him in the hog pen?" Some churches would have gone up to that boy and said, "Let us fill out your name right here. What's your name, son?" We've got other members still in the hog pen.

The father wanted the boy saved, but he never had to climb into the hog pen to save him. Unless we are willing to give up our calves, and have revival in our hearts, we are not going to see Holy Spirit, heaven-sent revival in our generation.

THE DEVIL IS DEALT DEFEAT

How is the devil defeated when revival comes? His lies are spotted. He says rebellion is right, but it's not. His likeness is seen. The devil's likeness is self-righteousness. Lucifer was a high creature in heaven, just like the older brother. His sin was trying to step up, not step down. His was a sin of arrogance and haughtiness.

Not only were the devil's lies spotted; his likeness seen, but his life-style was spurned. He said, "I'll not be in the hog pen anymore. I will arise and go to my father." I know many people who are in sin, but they don't live in any hog pen. Listen to me, if we live in a mansion without Jesus Christ, we live in a hog pen. The only life worth living is the life for Christ.

We need to be praying for revival in America. Then, when revival comes, we will see a new America, a new church, and a new people.

5
The Battle of Building

Nehemiah 4:17-18 teaches:

> They which builded on the wall, and they that bare burdens, with those that laded, every one with one of his hands wrought in the work, and with the other hand held a weapon. For the builders, every one had his sword girded by his side, and so builded. And he that sounded the trumpet was by me.

It is most interesting to note that when the wall of Jerusalem was built, the people had an instrument of war in one hand and an instrument for building in the other. May we find that as we build, not only buildings, but ourselves in Christian character and discipline, that we need, not only to have the instrument of construction, but an instrument of *destruction* as well. We must have the kind of people who know how to be aggressive in the battle for Christ, and who have a weapon of war against the forces of darkness.

Usually the sports personality who excels is the one who puts in the long hours of additional practice. The one who makes the A in school is the one who burns the midnight oil and makes the effort. The one who achieves is almost always the person who pays an extra price for that achievement. It is

so in every walk of life. Struggle almost inevitably comes before success.

A doctor comes out of a room and the family eagerly looks into his eyes, and he says, "Your dad is putting up a good fight." Why was their dad putting up a good fight? He was struggling so he might live and maintain himself. In every walk of life where there is battle, where there is struggle, and where there is effort, there is a goal of achievement, a desire to overcome mediocrity, and to reach the area of excellence. In every sphere of life that is true.

A man once told me that he wrestled seven hours to catch one fish. Yet, I have seen people go into a bait shop, buy a small net, and scoop up a half-dozen fish. It all depends on what you are after. The man wrestled seven hours for a marlin. The net scooped up minnows.

Recently on a commercial aircraft all of the "no-smoking" area was taken, so I had to sit in the back with the smokers. The roar of the engines was extremely loud on that 727. The motors were struggling. They were making an effort. While I was seated there in comfort, there was something outside my window working and moving for me. That was an effort for achievement. Had the motor stopped, the plane would have gone down. In every endeavor of life, the effort and the struggle is for achievement, accomplishment, and success.

Why is it that most churches are not evangelistic? Why are most churches small, fault-finding, or critical? The answer is obvious and simple. It is because everytime a church builds, there is a battle. A leader should not do what is comfortable. He is to launch out—to go forward. There is never a time in the history of a church when that church should build walls around what it already has. It must always be on the building avenues of greater achievement. A church that decides to build walls around what it already has will be a church that loses. God has only one gear for a church. That is forward.

After being in Babylon for seventy years, Nehemiah re-

THE BATTLE OF BUILDING

turned to Jerusalem and noticed that the walls were demolished. In some places the walls were only damaged, but where they were demolished, he encouraged the people to build.

As the chapters unfold, we find Nehemiah having a difficult time with his antagonists. He had enemies, of course. Every true servant of God does. He said to this workers, "I want you brick-layers to have a trowel in one hand and a hachet in the other hand. As you are spreading that mortar with one hand, you can clobber an Ammonite with the other. I want you carpenters to have a hammer in one hand, and a sword in the other." This is the way they began to build the wall. They had an instrument of construction in one hand and a weapon of war in another hand. Please notice in this passage the kind of attitude that Nehemiah had to face as the wall was being built.

THE BATTLE WITH THE HEARERS WITH THE HANG-UPS

Let's look at some of the battles of building. For one thing, we have to battle the hearers with hang-ups. Nehemiah 4:1 states, "But it came to pass, that when Sanballat heard that we builded the wall, he was wroth, and took great indignation, and mocked the Jews." Then verse 7 says, "But it came to pass, that when Sanballat, and Tobiah, and the Arabians, and the Ammonites, and the Ashdodites, heard that the walls of Jerusalem were made up, and that the breaches began to be stopped, then they were very wroth."

It's amazing that part of those who hold the church back are "hearers." "Guess what I heard!" Funny, we never have to guess because they always tell us.

I have heard some funny ones since I have been pastoring. What would we have thought of the Apostle Paul if he had said, "I heard that Jesus Christ is adequate for life. I heard that he would die on the cross. I heard that he would resurrect."

However, the thing that bothers me about a "hearer" is

simply this—God does not want us to be folks who tell what we have *heard*. He wants us to be people who share what we *know*. The thing I learned about Paul was that he *knew* that Christ was an experience in his life. He *knew* that Christ had died upon the cross. He *knew* that Christ had risen from the grave, because on the road to Damascus he had seen that blinding light and he had been changed by the power of God. If we major on what we *know,* such as the salvation that is in Christ, that of which we are assured, we won't have time to spread what we have *heard*. We would be found sharing with people what we *know* through Christ Jesus.

Be careful of people who say, "Have you heard?" God has a weapon for that, and the weapon is prayer. We need to pray for some folks. Notice what they prayed in verse 4, "Hear, O our God; for we are despised: and turn their reproach upon their own head, and give them for a prey in the land of captivity." God has a weapon for the hearers with hang-ups.

THE BATTLE OF THE COWARDS WHO ARE CRITICAL

Now, let's look at the second kind of person we have to battle when we build. Not only are there the hearers with hang-ups, but there are the cowards who are critical. Look in verse 3, "Now Tobiah the Ammonite was by him, and he said, Even that which they build, if a fox go up, he shall even break down their stone wall."

The thing I want us to notice is the phrase "by him." It is a shame, but some people have no reputation other than the identification they have with someone else. Tobiah is never referred to unless Sanballat is also mentioned. Tobiah was the little, crouching, deceitful man who was always the shadow of Sanballat. Tobiah was the kind of fellow who stuck his head out for just a moment, and said, "Yeah, me too." He was a coward and he was critical.

In chapter 2:10 and 2:19 he is referred to as a "servant."

THE BATTLE OF BUILDING

He thought he was something. A person often criticizes a program because he knows if he supports the program and that program achieves, he will have to pay a price to be involved. Instead of him truthfully saying, "I don't want to build that program because I will have to give money," they will say, "We are big enough. We have done all we need to do. God has been so good to us—let us just count the blessings that we have."

One time Mary burst an alabaster box of perfume upon the blessed Lord Jesus, and Judas said, "That was wrong. We could have given that to the poor." Is there any place in the Bible where we find Judas ever doing one thing for the poor? Judas wasn't concerned that the perfume could be sold and that money given to the poor. He knew that if someone else was that much in love with Jesus and that deeply committed to Christ, then maybe he ought to be. He didn't want anyone else completely committed to Christ because he wasn't ready to be that committed. We must sometimes look beyond what a person says to see what they are really saying. Tobiah said, "Oh, it's a weak wall."

Simon Peter jumped out of a boat (in Mark 6) and began to walk across the water. The disciples said, "Oh, no, Simon. You are making an idiot out of yourself. Stay in the boat with us." That's always the language of a coward. "Stay in the boat with us. Stay in the boat of apathy, of lethargy, of complacency." However, Simon Peter, by faith, walked on the water.

Paul and Barnabas went on a missionary journey, and carried a young preacher, John Mark, with them. The young man had plenty of zeal for Christ, but more zeal than real dedication. They reached the mission field, and were lying on the bare earth for a bed. Then the young preacher said to Paul and Barnabas, "I think we should go back." John Mark happened to be the nephew of Barnabas, and he said, "Uncle Barnabas, I think Paul is a fanatic. Let's go back. Those Gen-

tiles are not going to hear us. They don't want to hear the gospel. Let's go back, Uncle Barnabas."

John Mark didn't have any idea whether or not the Gentiles would be receptive, but he was scared to go. Finally, he went back home. This caused Paul and Barnabas to split up, and Paul later teamed up with Silas. John Mark turned a coward because he refused to pay the price of his missionary commitment. Thankfully, he later became a profitable servant and even helped Paul during his imprisonment. We don't need to become a coward or become critical. Cowards are always critical.

THE BATTLE WITH THE DOWNERS OF DISCOURAGEMENT

Let's now look at the third kind we must battle when we build. Not only are there the hearers with hang-ups, and the cowards who are critical, but there are the downers of discouragement.

Notice verse 10, "And Judah said, The strength of the bearers of burdens is decayed, and there is much rubbish; so that we are not able to build the wall."

Every word that he spoke was negative. Without faith, it is impossible to please God. We are able to do anything God wants us to do by his might.

Every now and then someone says to me, "Oh, Preacher, we just don't have the money." "Well," I say to them, "The money is here. We have it." But, the thing we are going to have to wrestle with is this—is my commitment as big as the vision of my church? Sometimes people say that the church is getting too big. What they mean is that the church has a bigger dedication than the person who is doing all the talking. The reason we work and ask for money is for one cause! It is so the Great Commission of Jesus Christ might somehow be fulfilled on this earth.

Let us never be so concerned about saving our time, our

THE BATTLE OF BUILDING

money, and our energy that we don't make an impact for God. There are thousands of churches around this world that are doing virtually *nothing*. Let's be so willing to pay the price—whatever it is—that we will shake this world for Christ and give Satan a headache. Let's put Christ upon the throne of everything we do.

Notice the downers of discouragement. One fellow was sent to the Congo, and he came back because he was sent to sell shoes. He said to his boss, "You are crazy. They don't even wear shoes." They sent another fellow and he said, "Praise God, there sure are a lot of prospects down here." It's all a matter of attitude and perspective.

One man wanted to sell milking machines in a place in Iowa. He went by a house one day and said, "I believe I can sell a milking machine here." His friend replied, "No, you can't. That man only has one cow. He doesn't have much money. You should sell a milking machine to man with a dozen or more cows." Pretty soon the man came out of the house smiling, but without his milking machine. His friend asked, "Are you telling me that you sold that man with one cow a milking machine?" He said, "Yes, but not only that, I took his cow for a down payment!"

Attitude is the important thing. He believed. He wasn't a downer. My dear friend, faith is not belief regardless of evidence. Faith is commitment in spite of the costs. We notice in this passage what a great commitment Nehemiah had, even in the face of the battle. Don't think it's going to be easy. There are going to be those who have the wrong attitude. But, praise the Lord, God is going to have the victory.

THE BATTLE WITH THE HATEFUL WHO HINDER

Fourth, there are the people who are hateful. It's the hateful who hinder God's work. There are many ways to hinder the Lord's work. Jesus said, "He who does not gather with me scattereth abroad." Is your personal vision as big as your

church's commitment? I hope it is. I think the cruelest thing that Jesus ever said was to Simon Peter. He said, "One day I am going to die and I'm going to bleed, crucified on the cross." Simon Peter said, "No, Lord." Jesus turned around and said, "Satan, get thee behind me."

He said that because Simon Peter's commitment stopped a bit short of total commitment. He had about 90 percent commitment, but when it came time for Peter to understand that to follow Christ may indeed mean the cross or shed blood, he said, "Oh no, Lord. Surely not."

It is so easy for a person to become hateful about the demands made upon him. Or even still, to become fault-finding. God doesn't ask for equal amounts. He asks for equal sacrifice. It's the hateful who hinder.

The Bible observes that they became very, very wroth. The first weapon God has against the hearers is prayer. The second weapon he has against the cowards who are critical is the Bible. To the downers of discouragement, it is the word of faith. The Bible says that he simply encouraged them to have faith. That's God's weapon against the downers. What is God's weapon against the hateful? It is diligence.

After this the Bible says in verse 9, "Nevertheless we made our prayer unto our God, and set a watch against them day and night, because of them." Isn't "nevertheless" a wonderful word?

THE BATTLE AGAINST THE NOBLES WHO DO NOTHING

Let's look at the fifth kind of person we have to battle to build. These are the nobles who do nothing.

Nehemiah 3:5 says, "And next unto them the Tekoites repaired; but their nobles put not their necks to the work of their Lord." Isn't that interesting!! They wanted to be big shots. However, God said that to enter into the kingdom of heaven, one must become as a little child. Some people want to be

THE BATTLE OF BUILDING

royal, but not loyal. Some people want to be like a mannequin in a department store window, "Look at me. Look at me." They stand aloof and apart. They want to be the judge of all that is going on. Those are the nobles who do nothing.

The nobles don't necessarily hurt you by sins of commission. They hurt you be sins of neglect. The noble says, "Well, well. I'm going to evaluate this whole program. We don't believe in making a commitment. We just believe in giving as God leads."

Be very careful at this point. Because if one did that, they would have to give everything they had. If we give as God leads, we will give more than twenty percent. When we give as God leads, we give all.

Don't be a part of the nobles who do nothing. They are so *important* that they are of no value. There are certain personal attributes one can have that are absolutely worthless, especially under particular circumstances. We don't need the nobles who do nothing. We don't need the hearers who hinder. We need the people who have a burning soul for God who realize that the only hope for this wicked world is Jesus Christ, and not only believe that with their heads, but believe it with their hearts and souls—and are willing to give their time, energies, and monies so the building might be built and the soul might be won and the gospel might be preached. We need people who will rise up and build the work of God!

THE BATTLE WITH THE FRAGILE WHO FEAR

There are also the fragile who fear. Verse 12 of chapter 4 reports, "And it came to pass, that when the Jews which dwelt by them came, they said unto us ten times, From all places whence ye shall return unto us they will be upon you."

Have you ever known the ten-time talker? They have to tell you at least ten times how bad things are. They are the fragile people who are always afraid. God also has a weapon for this kind of person. The weapon for fear is unity.

Verses 14 and 15 state, "And I looked, and rose up, and said unto the nobles, and to the rulers, and to the rest of the people, Be not ye afraid of them: remember the Lord, which is great and terrible, and fight for your brethren, your sons, and your daughters, your wives, and your houses. And it came to pass, when our enemies heard that it was known unto us, and God had brought their counsel to nought, that we returned all of us to the wall, every one unto his work."

You and I can conquer if we will join hands and hearts. God is concerned that we all do our work *together*. That's God's weapon against fear.

Years ago a girl was lost in a huge field. For hours the people of the community looked for that little child. Finally, when it became midnight, they still could not locate that little girl, even with lights all over the field. A man and woman cried because their daughter was lost. A man finally said, "Let's all join hands and go down one side of the pasture and up the other side. We'll sweep the field until we have covered every inch of it. We will join hands and go together." They joined hands and not long after that, they found the body of that little girl. That mother and father came to the broken body of that child.

The father looked up the sky and said, "Oh, God! Why didn't we join hands a little bit earlier?" That little girl might be alive today had they joined hands a little bit sooner.

Join hands with each other and let God work a miracle. Let's battle for the building of the kingdom of God on this earth. Let's do it now!

6
Revival or Regret

King David was no ordinary spiritual man. He was a man who accomplished grand things politically, financially, and materially. Even though Solomon received credit for the Temple, the Temple really belonged to David. It was his idea, and it was he who started what we now know as Solomon's Temple. He was a man of unbelievable accomplishment, a man of unusual intellect, a man who throughout his life could point to the constant intervention of God.

Many of us could stand and testify, "When I chose that particular school, God was in that choice; when I married that woman, God was in that choice; when we had those children, it was a blessing of God; when I applied for and got that job, I saw that God was in it. God in his wisdom was in that choice."

Many could say that throughout their lives, God has been there in various events. God has been evidenced. He has been seen.

David was that kind of man. Throughout the events and the occasions of his life, it seemed that everywhere he turned, there was God. God was there in unbelievable fashion.

In his youth, as a teenager, when he was chosen to be king, he was God's choice. He was indeed a man of God. But it sounds paradoxical to comment that here was a man "after God's own heart"—here was a godly man—here was a man of God, and yet he is also known as a murderer, a killer, an

adulterer, an evil man. There seems to be something radically wrong about that statement. Nevertheless, it is a true statement.

David the man of God and David the murderer were one and the same person! The man chosen of God. There are some lessons from David's story that are of vital importance to help every Christian avoid some pitfalls into which David fell. How could such a fall happen to a man of God? How could it happen to a man who was a spiritual man, a man of great valor, a man of prayer, a man who loved the Scriptures, a man of poetry, a man who used to strum the harp and make songs and hymns unto God? How did it happen that a man of unparalleled devotion to God became a murderer? How?

DON'T TAKE YOUR EYES OFF GOD

The painful fact is that the holiest people of all, with their eyes turned from God for one fleeting moment, can bring regrettable sin into their lives. David was a man who encountered a giant. The Israelites were terribly afraid of that giant. All the Israelites thought he was too big to strike down, but David thought he was too big to miss! David went out to fight the giant and embedded a stone in the giant's forehead. Then he walked over to that giant, jumped on his chest, which lifted him about six feet higher, took the sword out of the giant's sheath, and severed the giant's head from his body. He picked the head up by the hair, and dragged the head back to the forefront of the battle, announcing, "There has been a victory won for the Lord God of Israel."

There was a time when David met a ferocious lion. Yet he was victorious over the lion. And there is no more glorious story in the Bible of one man's love for another than the story of David and Jonathan. They loved each other and shared with each other, and their hearts seemed to beat for each other. It is a story that inspires all of us to be better friends to

each other. David was a friend to Jonathan, and Jonathan a friend to David.

Psalms, the biggest book in all of the Bible, is filled with the wisdom, insight, and sensitivity of David, for he was a man who knew God. He was a man who sought God, prayed to God, wrote about God, and dedicated songs to God. He was a man who had God in his life throughout all of his days.

David the murderer? How could that happen? It happens when a man, in his Christian life, grows and grows and then sits down upon what he thinks he has done. This was David. All of David's life God had intervened. Then he became king, and he somehow sat down and quit being what he should have been.

In Jeremiah 2:13 God looked at his people and said, "For my people have committed two evils; they have forsaken me the fountain of living waters, and hewed them out cisterns, broken cisterns, that can hold no water."

People in West Texas know what a cistern is. A cistern is not a well. A well is something that has a supply of water from the earth, but a cistern is nothing but a container that collects rainwater which runs off the house.

God said to the people of Israel that they had become cisterns or collectors, but that they no longer could hold the water. They were stagnant. They leaked. If a person is not careful, he will climb the spiritual ladder of stardom and sit down, exactly as David did. He will turn his eyes from God for only a moment and then regrettable, hideous sin will enter his life.

How does a person turn his eyes from God? A person turns his eyes from God when he ceases to participate in those things that point his eyes toward God. That's how one gets his eyes off God.

Most churches have a deacon or two that are no longer "active." They turned their eyes from God. But how did they

do it? It happens when a person avoids those things that point his eyes and his life toward God. He begins to take the Bible less seriously than before. He begins to avoid times of prayer and devotional life and silence before God. He begins to miss prayer meeting. That's nearly always the first service abandoned. Then, he begins to miss Sunday night services; then soon it's Sunday morning. Soon he buys himself a camper, then a cabin on the lake. Before you know it, he has to miss every other Sunday. By then, he has turned his eyes from those exercises that would usually point him toward God, and he finds himself looking more at things than he does at God.

That's what happened in the life of David. Second Samuel 11:4-6 relates that David was up on his rooftop, and he gazed next door and saw a woman named Bathsheba taking a bath. When he saw Bathsheba, he wanted to commit immorality with her. He sent his messengers, and they brought the woman to David's house. When David committed immorality with her, he sent her back home.

However, he then began to think to himself, *I want that beautiful woman.* When he thought that, his mind began to dwell upon it, and his lust began to have unstoppable play.

Soon he desired to have the woman so much that he sent her husband, Uriah the Hittite, and ordered him put in the front lines of battle in order for him to be killed. Sure enough, he was killed. Afterward, David added Bathsheba to his harem of wives.

How would a man ever get so caught up in lust like that? David the man of God became David the murderer. How does a man look upon a woman's body in lust to such a degree that he would kill her husband in order to get her? That only happens when a godly man turns his eyes away from the matters that put his eyes upon God. I don't care how spiritual a person is. It doesn't matter how many payments one has had for God or how God has been good to him in the past or even how God has blessed him in his life.

There is never a time in a Christian's life when that Christian can be "at ease in Zion." There is never a period when we can quit reading the Bible. There is never a season when we can afford to neglect prayer. There is never a moment when we can quit soul-winning or services or when we can take our eyes off of those things which are holy, righteous, and spiritual.

In one moment of spiritual laziness, there can come a temptation through which we will fall victim and will live all of the rest of our lives to regret it. There are preachers who will never preach again and, evangelists, gifted of God in evangelism, who have seen hundreds of people come down the aisle and respond to their message, who will never win another soul to Christ because of their sin. In spite of the fact that they were men of God and men upon whom God had put his hand and blessing, when they began to neglect holy and righteous things, in one moment of temptation, they were not strong enough to withstand. Like David, who desired for a woman to go to bed with him, they wanted something that wasn't right for them. In one moment, with their eyes somewhere else besides on God, their lives fell in ill repute.

If we could have interviewed King David the day before he looked upon Bathsheba with lust and asked him, "David, would you ever commit immorality or commit murder in order to get what you wanted?" David would have replied, "No, a thousand times no. I would never do anything like that." But the next day, he did exactly that.

When a person loses his spiritual focus, when he rivets his eyes on ambition, lust, a job, a position, or on anything other than God, he is in danger of tragedy and heartache. David turned his eyes from God for one fleeting moment, and he ruined a nation and hampered his life.

Isaiah 29:13 says, "Wherefore the Lord said, Forasmuch as this people draw near me with their mouth, and with their lips do honour me, but have removed their heart far from me

. . . ." David began to become too familiar with the sacred. It's easy to handle the Bible so loosely that it is no longer sacred to us. It's possible to see so many people baptized that it doesn't remain sacred. Some handle the Lord's Supper as though it were a time of refreshment. Some are so loose in church that when they walk in the doors, there is no longer a sense of awe or of God's holiness, presence, and power.

David started dealing with the things of the "church." When David went to church, he was given the best seat in the house. David heard what David wanted to hear preached because he could do away with the priest if he wanted to. He was the king! But he became so familiar with the sacred that there was no longer a majesty for him.

Judges 16:30 says that the presence of the Lord left Samson, and he didn't even know it! Because some have taken their eyes off God, God is no longer working with them. His presence and his power is not strong with them. Samson found it out only when he was put to a test. Some people have neglected the things of God and of righteousness. They have turned their backs on the things that are precious, holy, and right. Yet, they still think they are all right. When Samson was put to a test, he discovered that he no longer had any strength. If some are not careful, when the test comes to them they are going to fail and discover that they have taken their eyes off God. No one is too spiritual to backslide.

The best man that ever lived, according to Jesus, was John the Baptist. Jesus said that no man ever born was greater than John the Baptist. But when John the Baptist got in trouble, he said, "I don't even know whether or not Jesus is the Messiah."

After he wrote one Christian epistle after another, the Apostle Paul moaned in Romans 7 that the things he wanted to do, he didn't do, and the things that he shouldn't do, he discovered himself doing.

Simon Peter, who followed Jesus and upon whose face

Jesus built his church said, "I don't even know the man." Here are men who spent time after time with Jesus. One denied him; one cursed him; and one said he didn't even know if he were the Messiah. How could that happen? Because in every case those men were put under unbelievable tests, and somewhere in their lives they had gotten their eyes on being popular or on being accepted or on being loved. A man of God cannot have his eyes on anything other than God.

GOD NEVER APPROVED OF ANY PERSON'S SIN

David knew a lot of evil things. David knew it was wrong to talk in church. He knew it was wrong to go into the holy of holies. But after all, David was king. You see, David stumbled because God doesn't approve of any man's sin. Whoever one is, God does not approve of sin. David perhaps thought, *Well, after all, I am king! One more woman won't hurt. I have a right to do this.*

If we are not careful, we will begin to classify what is sinful. Many years ago churches had what was known as "church discipline." People would be kicked out of church for committing immorality. There is some merit about keeping the Bride of Christ clean and pure. But church discipline can be wrong because, if a church disciplines people on the basis of their sins, pretty soon people who find splinters in the eyes of others will be kicking people out while they have 2 by 4s in their own eyes!

Jesus declared that it is not what goes into a man's mouth that fouls him up, but rather what comes out that is sinful. We must understand that Jesus Christ never approved of any man's sins. A man should abstain from smoking or drinking. But, just because one hasn't done these outward things doesn't mean he is a saint.

David thought that since he was the king he "could get by with murder"! More harm has been done in Baptist churches by the tongue than by the bottle. There are not many Baptist

churches where the bottle is the major problem. But most Baptist churches have had serious problems with the tongue. To condemn people for a bunch of sins is often to begin to look at others and take our attention off of "self." In fact, it is probably just as bad to be talking about people's sins than to commit the sins.

We must be careful lest we become so condemning and self-righteous that we will be more like those Jesus condemned than like Jesus himself. In Luke 13:3-5 a group of Pharisees came to Jesus and told him about a lot of evil things, but Jesus was not disturbed. They said, "Lord, we thought you were really going to get upset with these incidents." Jesus stood back, pointed his finger at that group, and said, "No, but I say unto you that unless you repent, you shall all likewise perish." He knows that most of us are too eager to confess the faults of another when we need to confess our own.

There are so many unhappy, grouchy people with bad attitudes. There is no sin that a man can have that God approves of. There should be a sign over every Christian church and over Christian life, "No pets allowed." No pet grudges, no pet prejudices, no pet gossip, no pet attitudes. We must get all "pets" out of our lives and bow down before Him who is holy and righteous.

David really backslid and when he did, he encouraged the enemy. Second Samuel 12:14 relates, "Howbeit, because by this deed thou hast given great occasion to the enemies of the Lord to blaspheme . . . ." Nathan said, "David, it is not only bad that you have sinned, but you have committed murder. You have robbed a woman of her rightful place with her husband. You have caused the people who hate God to rejoice. David, you need to hate your own sin."

A church I know about fired their last four pastors. They had all kinds of tragedies and bad experiences in that church. People in town would talk about the bad things going on in that church. Every drunkard in that city talked about the

church. Everyone who wanted to talk about hypocrites would use that church as an illustration of why they didn't have to go to church. When a person commits sin and does things against God, or when he has a spirit and attitude he should not have and says things he shouldn't say, not only does it hurt him, but it encourages the work of the devil.

Nathan said, "David, you have given the people who hate the Lord a reason to rejoice. David, you have encouraged it. You have put fuel on the fire. You have given Satan a thrill."

When a person talks about people, it hurts God, but it helps the devil.

Churches, as the body of Christ, like never before must bind together in the spirit of the Lord and commit to him and to one another. We must say, "Lord, make us pure and make us right, and encourage us to be the people that you want us to be. May we never say anything that would give the people who would destroy the great work of God's church reason to be happy."

If one does commit sin, there is always a place to confess. There is a place to receive forgiveness. In Genesis 35:1 God told Jacob to go and build that altar at Bethel. God was saying, "Jacob, I will be with you. I shall restore you."

Jesus wants us to be right. He wants us to be loving. He wants us to be sweet-natured. He wants us to be forgiving. He wants us to be understanding. He wants us to be soul-winners. He wants us to be a people of prayer, Bible reading, and of deep devotional life. But if we stumble, we can still remember that the "Lord is our shepherd."

David looked over and saw a woman he wanted. One thing stood in his way. His name was Uriah. Many people are just like David, looking at what they want, but there remains one thing in the way. That which stands in the way is none other than the Lord.

David had two choices. David could have said, "I want that woman, but since her husband stands in between me and

her, I will not have that woman. That woman belongs to him. I will respect God's design. I will honor the fact that the woman belongs to him. I will respect that relationship." That's one choice David had. The other choice he had was, "I want her more than I want to do what is right. Therefore, I am going to jerk him out of the way. I am going to kill him in order that I might go and embrace what I want."

Jesus stands in our way. He stands in our way of going to hell. We can say, "Jesus, get out of my way. I prefer to do what I want to do. Because I am lost and turning my back upon every effort to save me, I am simply saying, 'I want to go to hell.' Therefore, Jesus get out of my way. Jesus, I want to do everything I want to do. I want to fulfill my lusts. I want to fulfill my ambitions. I want to do what I want to do. I want to feel like I feel." A person can't turn his back upon someone and love him at the same time. To drift away and come dangerously close to committing regrettable sin is possible unless Jesus is allowed to get between the Christians and that heinous sin that will destroy their lives.

What will it be? Revival or regret!

7
Four Things God Does Not Know

In reading Psalms the concept which seems to be paramount is the psalmists' respect for the Name and the Person of God. How unfathomable were the awe and wonder they had for God.

The psalmists would sing that their God is above the kings of the earth. He stands literally upon the circle of the earth. God is our fortress. God is our might. God is our courage. And he is greater than all others. There is none other like unto God.

Looking through the Psalms, you would find a golden thread of unbelievable respect for the name of God. When Hebrew scribes were translating the biblical text, they would come to the name *Yahweh* (which is the Hebrew translation for the word *Jehovah*. We have made it the word *God*) and would put down their used pen or stylus, write the word *God* with a new one, then throw away that one, and pick up another to begin again translating the text. When they came to the word *Yahweh* again, they would secure a fresh pen to write his name. This was because of their awesome respect for God. They refused to write any other word with the same pen with which they had written the name of God.

We must return to that awe of the holiness of God. Even in our Christian worship, we need a new awe, a new reverence, and a new respect for the righteousness, holiness, and great-

ness of God himself. There are many words with which we describe God. We call God omnipotent, which means all-powerful. We speak about the omnipresent God, which means all-present. Then we call God omniscient. This means he is all-knowing. He is a powerful, mighty, courageous, unequaled, unparalleled being. He is God of this universe, and unto him there is none even similar to what he is and who he is.

With all of these thoughts in mind about God himself, what I am saying is that this wonderful, omnipotent, omniscient, omnipresent God has no comparison; there is no one even close to him.

However, even in the light of all of this, there are four things that God does not know. Before this wonderful God the psalmists would bow their heads in reverence and respect, speaking words that flowed with eloquence and power. Yet, this God, as wonderful, great, and unequaled as he is, does not know *four things*. What could they be? What are the things this great God of ours does not know?

GOD DOES NOT KNOW A SIN HE DOES NOT HATE

First, God does not know a sin he doesn't hate. God hates sin. Do you know what sin is? In short, sin is rebellion toward God and disobedience against God. When you talk about the "wages of sin" being death, it is interesting to note that the word *wages* literally means "rotten meat." Sin is like meat from the grocery store. It looks good, we carry it home, and think it will really be good for us. But if that meat is rotten it will make a bad taste in our mouths and even make us ill. Sin is a pleasure for a season—then it always brings forth death. God hates sin.

There was a time in the Bible when the Ark of the Covenant was to be moved, and God said, "If anyone touches the ark, they will be destroyed." Some men were carrying the ark, and all of a sudden they became overloaded with the weight

FOUR THINGS THAT GOD DOES NOT KNOW

of the ark and it tipped. There was a man standing nearby. He didn't want that ark to tip over and fall on the ground. He had far too much respect for the things of God to let the ark of God fall. He had heard what God said about anyone touching it. But he must have thought, *In this case God doesn't want the ark to fall on the ground.* So, he put up his hands, and when he put up his hands to stop the ark from falling, he was immediately killed. His name was Uzzah (2 Sam. 6:7). God kept his promise. God hates sin. God hates disobedience. God is repulsed by the rebellion of a person who tries to find a better way to do something other than the dictates, words, and promises of God.

There were some people in the Old Testament who decided to become immoral. God asked those people to change, but they wouldn't. Recorded in Numbers 25 let's examine what God did about it.

> And Israel abode in Shittim, and the people began to commit whoredom with the daughters of Moab. And they called the people unto the sacrifices of their gods: and the people did eat, and bowed down to their gods. [Not only were they immoral, but they were idolatrous.] And Israel joined himself unto Baalpeor: and the anger of the Lord was kindled against Israel. And the Lord said unto Moses, Take all the heads of the people, and hang them up before the Lord against the sun, that the fierce answer of the Lord may be turned away from Israel. And Moses said unto the judges of Israel, Slay ye every one of his men that were joined unto Baalpeor. And, behold, one of the children of Israel came and brought unto his brethren a Midianitish woman in the sight of Moses, and in the sight of all the congregation of the children of Israel, who were weeping before the door of the tabernacle of the

congregation. And when Phinehas, the son of Eleazar, the son of Aaron the priest, saw it, he rose up from among the congregation, and took a javelin in his hand; And he went after the man of Israel into the tent, and thrust both of them through, the man of Israel, and the woman through her belly. So the plague was stayed from the children of Israel.

Some think that we must be kinder to those who commit sin. What we really need to do with those who commit sin is be more truthful with them. We need to preach God's Word straight at them. The Israelite man and Midianite woman were thrust through. God was teaching them to know that he is holy and of righteous standards. God will not bend for anyone's tradition. God will not sway for anyone's needs on a particular day. God will not compromise concerning lusts or that which satisfies one's hunger for whatever the world has to offer. God doesn't know a sin he doesn't hate. You name the sin. God hates it. It is sin God hates. We don't become sinners by sinning; we sin because we are sinners.

It is our nature to sin as it is the nature of a dog to bark or a cat to meow. One does not have to spank a child to get him to do bad. It's amazing how they do that all by themselves. One has to spank and discpline children to make them do good. That sinful old nature of ours will make us do things we should not do. It is *that* sinful nature which God hates.

A person may be self-righteous with all kinds of sins in his own life. But he may not even notice those sins because he is too busy pointing his finger at the sins of others. Beware! It is not just alcoholism, adultery, or pornography that God hates. God hates sin—period. All inclusive. Anything that is contrary to a holy and righteous God, he hates.

There was a man and woman named Ananias and Sapphira who lied to the Holy Spirit. All of a sudden they were stricken dead.

God hates sin for one basic reason. God hates sin because sin is in conflict with the nature of God. It is the nature of God to be holy and righteous. He knows that sin drove Adam and Eve out of the Garden of Eden. He knows that sin is what made Cain pick up a club and beat his brother Abel to death. That's against the nature of God. God is love and righteousness. He hates sin because it is against his nature.

God is our Father in heaven and he wants to protect us. It is amazing to see people blame God for things that he didn't have anything to do with. It is not God's fault when someone does not watch over their children when they play near the street. God's greatest concern is that we have health, happiness, light, and abundance. Therefore, it is against his nature for sin to be in this world, and he despises that.

As a father I am responsible for providing the physical needs of my three children. I am responsible for keeping our home generally in order and maintaining the upkeep and safety of the home. God as the Father in heaven wants us to be protected against everything bad that comes to us. It's frightening to see those who flirt with sin and live in rebellion against God.

A deacon related that he had been working with a girl who had many problems. She had been living with a man who was not her husband. The deacon asked her why she was doing that and she replied that the man provided a roof over her head and the heads of her children. The children's father had run away and the children had to eat. When asked why she wouldn't marry him, she replied, "Well, I don't think I love him enough to marry him. I just love him enough to live with him." The deacon scolded her for this attitude and she asked, "Oh, are you one of those folks who believe in the Ten Commandments?"

The muscle and the heart of this world are those people who *believe* in the Ten Commandments. The glue that holds this world together, that keeps it from flying apart in some kind

of insanity are those people who believe in the Ten Commandments and the words of Christ and the things of holiness and righteousness.

The life that is lived for Jesus Christ and the truths of the Bible is the life that is happy and whole. There is not one thing this stinking, old, dirty world has to offer that a person can't find better in Jesus Christ. This world is not even competition to Jesus Christ.

"The wages of sin is death, but the gift of God is eternal life through Jesus Christ our Lord" (Rom. 6:23). If it's rebellion against God in any way, God hates it. A man that loves his wife doesn't want to do things she hates. Much more, a Christian doesn't want to do things God hates, and God categorically hates sin.

GOD DOESN'T KNOW A SINNER HE DOESN'T LOVE

God hates lying, but he loves the liar. God hates murder, but he loves the murderer. God hates adultery, but he loves the adulterer. Everything that is sinful about man is hated and despised by God; but He loves us. He loves us so much that he sent his son to die in our place that we might have life.

If a person goes to the doctor and the doctor examines him and recommends that he should have a shot, the man usually doesn't accuse the doctor of condemning him. Very few would change doctors for being truthful about what was wrong with them.

A preacher is a spiritual doctor. He has to point out the illness, but the one who is ill must take the medicine. The doctor can't go to the drugstore and follow the patient home and give him the medicine. A preacher can only prescribe that God hates lying, sinning, and adulterous ways. But in the midst of all of that hatred there is another thing God does not know. He does not know a sinner he does not love.

Someone can go out on the street right now and shake his fist to heaven and shout, "God, I hate you. Take your Jesus

Christ and stuff him the other side of heaven someplace," and the voice from heaven will come back, "But, my child, I love you." The Bible says that God is love.

At a Convention during the Pastors Conference, I had asked a certain woman to be on the program. Twenty-one thousand people showed up to hear her. Outside, there were 200 homosexuals with various vulgar placards. One of them had a sign that said, "Jesus didn't die for my sins." As I looked at those people, I thought about what a wonderful God we have that would love those folks.

He hates the sin, but he loves the sinner. The only thing that keeps a man out of hell is the love of God. The only person who loves a homosexual is the person who will tell him he's perverted.

The best friend the homosexual ever had was the man who told him that homosexuality was a perversion and wrong and a sin against God. When a homosexual or an adulterer realizes it is wrong, he can repent of his sins and our loving God can change him and set his feet upon a rock and give him a sense of purpose and tranquility, instead of guilt.

Every year thousands of homosexuals commit suicide because they cannot cope with the perversion that has come into their lives. There is an avenue of being set free and finding new life. Some so-called intellectuals claim homosexuality is merely a sexual preference. That's like saying some people just prefer murder or child abuse or stealing. Are we as a society going to say, "Do whatever is your preference."? Some people prefer stupidity because they are stupid.

To change a person's preference, one must first change the person. The only way a sinner can ever be different is to say, "I am a sinner." To condone sin is to live with it the rest of our lives because a man will excuse it. Why? Because society has excused it. If society approves sin, it still doesn't mean God has approved it.

Some parents approve of their children's rebellion and are

creating a criminal for society someday. God does not approve of sin, but he approves of people. He loves the person. It cost him his Son upon the cross. He loves people more than we can ever imagine, and wants us to realize that we can be saved. He wants us to know that we can be different.

People always ask what they can do to be saved. There is nothing they can do to be saved. "Believe on the Lord Jesus Christ and thou shalt be saved," says the Bible (Acts 16:31). What one must do to be saved has already been done. Believing, accepting, receiving, and letting Christ be our own personal Lord and Savior saves us.

Some Iranian students engaged me in conversation. They stated they were Muslims and that they believed good people would go to heaven and bad people would go to hell. When asked if they were going to heaven, they said they were—because they were good. I asked how they were going to maintain that goodness. Muhammad taught many of the same teachings that Jesus taught, but the basic difference between Jesus and Muhammad was: Muhammad claimed to be a prophet pointing the way to God, but Jesus Christ is the Savior who payed for our sins. He claimed that when he was dying for us by substituting for our sins on the cross, he did it as God himself. Jesus was not a prophet of God like Muhammad. *Jesus was and is God.*

The first time I got those Iranian students' attention, I replied that Muhammad was a great teacher and prophet, but only Jesus was Savior. He died to take our place on the cross. Sins will either send us to hell, or we will allow Jesus to take hell for us. Only Jesus died so that we would not have to die—no one else could do that. He's our substitute, and he loves us.

It's hard for me to love child abusers, but God loves them. God even loves people with poor demented minds. I don't care how evil and rotten a person has been. Whatever a person has done, God still loves him.

GOD DOESN'T KNOW A BETTER SALVATION

There is only one avenue of salvation. That is through Jesus Christ.

"For God so loved the world that he gave his only begotten son" (John 3:16). "If thou shalt confess with thy mouth the Lord Jesus and believe in thine heart that God has raised him from the dead, thou shalt be saved" (Rom. 10:9). I cannot improve on that.

Some think that salvation is social involvement. I remember the labor of the PTA and band parents, but working in the concession stand won't usher you into heaven. Being a loyal community citizen won't get a person into heaven. There are people who go to church, PTA, country club, band parents' meeting, and the football quarterback club. Consequently merely church is another place for many, to go to, so a person will look like a good citizen. The church of Jesus Christ is not merely one among many things to which a person should give his attention. It is the number-one thing for a child of God.

Every now and then someone will remark to me, "Preacher, we have to give up our class because we are going to be involved in Little League baseball." Now, I'm grateful to God for those who work in Little League baseball. But if a Christian has to make a choice between God's house and anything of the world, friends, it had better not be the world. We had better have loyalty to God's house.

The events of the world succeed much more than the matters of God because God's so-called people are saying "No" to the church and "Yes" to the world. People become loyal to the world, thinking that they are community-minded. But no one has ever gone to heaven for what he has done for the community. Certainly there are other things to be done, but there are only so many hours in the day. Our first loyalty as Christians should be to God and his church. Other people can make a priority of the other things. While people try to work

their way in social involvement to be saved, God doesn't know anything about it.

Some people have another religion called "God-understands" religion. They say, "No, preacher, I've never been saved, but God understands." God does not understand! All that God understands is that only through Jesus Christ does a person go to heaven. Without Jesus Christ a person goes to hell. There is no excuse for anyone's particular case. There never has been an exception to that. God does not know a better way to be saved than through Jesus Christ and his blood on the cross.

The third religion people think will carry them to heaven is, "I know more than you think I know." They "know" what we do with the money at the church. They "know" about "those hypocrites." Many people are bowing before the altar of suspicion and criticism.

Do you think anyone is going to make it on that kind of "wonderful wisdom"? Do you think there is anyone in the world who knows more about the weakness of the church than a preacher of the gospel who has spent all of his life in churches? I not only know bad things about the church—I know bad things about me! While a person might stumble over me and some of these church members, no one will ever stumble over Jesus Christ. He is "the way, the truth, and the life" (John 14:6).

Imagine a fellow going to the doctor for an appendectomy and requesting a local anesthetic! The doctor would advise that being put completely under with anesthetic is the normal procedure. When questioned on why he was insisting on the local, the man might reply, "Well, I just want to tell you what to do." It is amazing how many people want to tell the minister, who has spent most of his life learning the Bible, that they, by their neglect and their unfaithfulness, somehow know more than he does. It's mind-blowing how their ignorance has

made them so wise! God has no better way for us to be saved than Jesus Christ. God knows no better way of salvation.

GOD DOES NOT KNOW A BETTER TIME THAN NOW TO BE SAVED

Last of all, *now* is the best time to be saved. Today is the day of salvation. "Now is the accepted time" (2 Cor. 6:2).

God says the brevity of life is so sure. Life is held by such a fragile thread. One reason a person needs to be saved now, no matter what his age, is because no one has the promise of another day.

Furthermore, Jesus Christ might come tonight. And most people think that when they reach the point of death that they will call their families to the bedside, fold their arms, read their will to the family, and tell them good-bye. It probably won't be that way at all.

Today is the day to be saved. Now is the accepted time. Many people alibi, "Not today," but what they are really saying is "No." When a person says, "not now" to Jesus, he is really saying, "Jesus, as far as right now is concerned you are a liar. Jesus, as far as right now is concerned, I don't want to have anything to do with your plan of salvation. Jesus, as far as right now is concerned, I reject you totally."

As far as God is concerned, to say "Not now," in God's eyes is saying "no" forever. For God knows you may not have another time. For some, God realizes that this is their last opportunity to be saved. It's a slap in the face of a Holy God to say, "God, You wait on me. I'll come around someday, maybe. If you are a good enough God, I'll come see you later."

God doesn't know a better time to be saved than right now. A person can bring happiness to heaven, happiness to loved ones, happiness to those around, by giving his heart and life to Jesus Christ. God doesn't know a better time.

8
The Gospel in Miniature

The Bible offers us incomparable passages of truth that deserve meticulous consideration. But the Bible also contains what appears to be "just a passing word," a phrase which, upon a glance, seems to be only a small portion of something more important.

Such a passing thought, yet with a profound message, is found in John 4:6, "Now Jacob's well was there. Jesus therefore, being wearied with his journey, sat thus on the well: and it was about the sixth hour."

Most people probably would not even notice this verse without understanding the history of it. However, there is a special message in this small phrase. "Now Jacob's well was there . . . ."

Many of us have probably received more in life by inheritance than we have ever worked for. As we look around and see our freedom, the massive highways, the parks, the protection afforded us by our government, and many other blessings, we realize that we are the inheritors of mighty and wonderful bounties.

It was the same with the children of Israel. The Bible records that they came in and lived in houses they had not built. They gathered from fields they had not planted. They took fruit from trees in orchards they had not planted. Therefore, the children of Israel, going into the Promised Land, became

the recipients of houses, fields, and lands they had not labored to receive. They gathered vegetables and goods from a land they had not plowed.

Remember the passage which says, "Now Jacob's well was there . . . . "? When this story was written, Jacob's well had been there 1700 years. The well has now been there almost four thousand years and still supplies water and refreshment to all who come there!

Perhaps in light of the longevity of Jacob's well, there are tremendous lessons about building something solid. The well is still a tribute to Jacob that continues to honor him.

BUILD UPON WHAT WILL ENDURE

In order to build solid, one must always build upon that which shall endure. Jacob's work has apparently endured.

It's possible to tell the character of a person by the work he does. My father employed a particular man to change the oil and filter on his car. Dad always hired the same man. He did this for about three years until he had motor trouble and discovered that the man had not actually changed the oil or filter for three years! When he finally discovered the man's work, he learned something about the man's character. His character was obviously bad.

If a Christian doesn't produce many souls for Jesus, there is something wrong with that Christian's character. If a believer's life doesn't produce life in others that esteem the name of Jesus, then by the very fact that there is no fruit or outward evidence coming from that life, there is something wrong with that Christian's character.

In recommending Timothy to Philippi, Paul said that the proof of him was "he has served with me well." Proof of Christian character is not that we love to sing "those old gospel songs" or that we really get excited when we hear "good preachin'." There is more to it than that.

When we stand before God, he will examine our work and

thereby will reveal our character. God does not examine character, for he knows us inside and out. God looks at our works and then he determines our character.

The Bible indicates, not by their character ye shall know them, but "by their fruits" (Matt. 7:16).

There is no such thing as a good, wonderful, consecrated, dedicated, Spirit-filled, Christ-like "do-nothing." If one doesn't have sterling, wonderful works, then he must not have a wonderful, sterling character.

Notice something about Jacob. His character was indicated by his work. To find lazy work is to find a lazy person. To find diligent work is to find a diligent person. It was no doubt difficult for Jacob to build that well. The well was ninety feet deep, eight feet in diameter, and dug through almost solid rock. That would not be an easy well to dig today, and imagine how difficult it was to drill four thousand years ago!

Jacob must have thought at some time; *Well, I could build this more cheaply and cut corners on the stone. We could be a little sloppy and cheap as we shape and mold these stones with which to build this well.* That might have entered Jacob's mind. In fact, it could have entered his mind not to build a well at all.

The tribesmen before Jacob had not cared to build a well. They were like the Bedouins. The Bedouins consumed the fowl, flesh, and the fish, and then everybody had an empty dish! They brought their cattle in, the cattle took to the pasture, and nibbled away at the grass until they had consumed the roots. They drank in the ponds until every pond was absolutely bone dry. The Bedouins then picked up their goods after the cattle had eaten all of the grass. After they had come into a land, they left the land without grass or water.

The Bedouins are still doing that today. They are people who come and take and leave. I am sure it must have entered the mind of Jacob time and again to come into the world, take and leave; but he built something that has lasted four thou-

sand years. He decided that what he did was going to be a work that would endure.

To be a faithful steward of what God has given, one must exercise profound wisdom. It is doubtful that every time Jacob built one of those stones that he thought he was doing a mighty work. He just wanted to do that good work. Jacob had heard that the Messiah was going to come, but he probably never thought of Jesus drinking at that well. He was wiser than he even knew by doing his task right.

A lot of groups today talk about witnessing. There's not much credit for those witnessed to who never walk the aisles or be baptized or become excited about the Lord. Witnessing is not something to hear about—it is something to see. That's where it really counts. That's what God is concerned with—to really love lost souls is to want them in God's house and serving God.

A man related that when he was raising his nine children, they had the childhood diseases. They grew up into teenagers and rebelled. One of them was playing in nightclubs. The man didn't think any of his children would amount to anything. He felt he was making all kinds of mistakes. But now six of his boys are preachers, and one is an active deacon and layman. His daughters have married great Christian men.

He said, "You know, I just didn't realize I was doing so many things right." When asked what he had done, he said, "When they disobeyed, I beat the 'day-lights' out of them. Then, when we both got through crying, I read them the Bible. I had to get their attention."

Parents shouldn't worry about the difficult times as long as they rear their children in the Lord. Don't relinquish one moment or compromise one moment. Stick to the Bible, and watch what will eventually happen in the life of that child. A parent is wise when he makes that child walk the line and do what the Bible says.

When I'm asked if my parents allowed me to grow up and

things of God. To see what God has done with them is to appreciate their total lives. They might be rough as a cob, and have many idiosyncrasies. But to back off and look at the total life, one will praise God. Even with those little, strange habits, God is using them mightily and gloriously. Stand back and look at the beauty of the sun and look at the beauty of the paintings that God has performed in lives.

Jacob was not without his reward. The reward of Jacob was, first of all, knowing he had done a good job.

Once a doctor, while sewing up a patient, said to a friend standing nearby, "This is my 'sleep stitch.' I need to put only thirteen stitches, but I always put fourteen because when I go home at night and wonder if I have done a good job in sewing the patient up, I always remember that I did one more than I had to do. Then I can go to sleep. That's my sleep stitch."

How well would we sleep if we thought about how much we had responded to God's work in our lives? How well would we sleep if we counted the souls that had come to know Jesus in the last six months through our church? If we are winning souls to Christ, whose aisles are they walking? Where is the quality of our work?

A pastor I know was ready to quit the ministry. He walked in one night, turned on the television, and saw my brother-in-law speaking on the subject of "When You Are Ready to Throw in the Towel." As that pastor listened, he bowed his face before God and said, "God, I am sorry I have been so selfish and self-centered." My brother-in-law related that he did not realize that a year ago what he had said on television had turned around the life and saved the ministry of a fellow preacher.

If we stay true to God's Word, and become a person of prayer; if we dedicate ourselves to believe in God no matter what, the work will take care of itself. The rewards and the joy will come forth from it. Jacob received his reward with so much good being done.

NEVER CEASE TO BE A BLESSING

To build solid means we must never cease to be a blessing. Imagine how that well reflected gratitude through the years! For seventeen centuries Jacob's well had provided water. Note what Revelation 14:13 says: ". . . and their works do follow them." It's rather frightening, isn't it?

Our works follow us in two ways. First, they follow us eternally because there will be consequences in heaven for what we do on earth. They follow us, second, in the fact that what we do in the earlier parts of our lives will influence others throughout all of the years. Have you ever really spoken harshly to someone and later needed their friendship? Don't you now wish you had been nicer? Our works *do* follow us. Jacob's work followed him to such an extent that he had provided water for seventeen hundred years.

A good, godly life is like the sun. The sun comes up in the morning, passes over us all day long, and it is not until the evening that we say, "Look at those beautiful hues of sunlight. Isn't the sun beautiful? Look how it sets there!" By and large, the sun is only appreciated at the beginning or closing of the day. But in the morning at the 10 o'clock hour and on through the day, the sun had been doing its job and providing warmth to everyone.

If one is really what he ought to be, he won't be totally appreciated until he reaches the sunset years. There will be appreciation along the way, but we will never have the total appreciation until we come to those lasting sunset years and someone says, "He did live a good life and bring warmth." If one comes extra close to an expensive oil painting, nothing but brush strokes can be seen clearly. But to back away from it, a beautiful picture can be seen. It's from the distance that life is truly appreciated.

Some of the greatest Christians I have known have many brush strokes when you come up close. Our God has had to work in them, scar them, discipline them, teach them the

may be an indication of something left undone in years gone by.

A preacher friend of mine was reminiscing recently as he looked into a crib and saw his little daughter. He began to think how she would grow up one day and take her little lunch pail and go to school. He thought of how she would graduate from high school and how proud they would be of her as she crossed the stage to receive that diploma. Then one day they would take her to a college campus and let her out on that strange campus. As he was daydreaming about these things, he became upset because he had remembered that his wife met him when he was a freshman in college.

He began to think about that little baby in the crib who would one day be going to college. He then realized that his daughter would probably some day marry. He said, "You know, I started thinking as I looked at my little baby there in the crib in all of her innocence. We were trying to raise her in the nurture and admonition of the Lord, but I got to wondering, *Where is the boy that she's going to marry someday when she goes off to college? What do his parents do? How do his parents feel about God? How have his parents responded to Christ? How are his parents loving the Lord? How are his parents committing themselves to Christ?*

That man said he wanted to go out and win everybody to Christ he could. He wanted to love every family he could, sacrifice everything he could to win every family in his community because he didn't want some ungodly parent to raise a boy that would marry his Christian daughter.

We must not stop witnessing, or tithing, or serving, or praying, or loving just because it doesn't affect us now. It might not affect us now, but for sure it will affect us forever throughout eternity. Your labor will come back to you. How horrible it would be to leave someone lost who might raise a boy who will marry the daughter of a Christian, and teach her exactly opposite of what she was taught all of her days. We must beware of what we instill in the lives of these little ones.

THE GOSPEL IN MINATURE

make up my own mind about religion, I answer in the affirmative. "They sure did. I could either go to church or I got a size 42 belt." Dad had a big waist, but he could get that belt off as quickly as if he were about four inches around the waist.

Children should not have a choice about whether they are going to serve God. If they choose not to serve God, it ought to be over their bruises! There certainly needs to be some lovingkindness, discipline, and understanding. But even though it might not be "Dr. Spock," as long as it meets the Word of God, the parent is probably wiser than he ever thought.

Charles Evans Hughes was the first president of the Northern (now American) Baptist Convention. He was also the chief justice of the Supreme Court. A Sunday School teacher, eighty years of age, was summoned to a platform where Hughes was giving his testimony for Christ on one occasion. Charles Evans Hughes had that eighty-year-old Sunday School teacher stand beside him and tell the people how he taught his Sunday School class in which Justice Hughes had been taught. The old man walked to the platform, trembling with age, stood erect for the occasion, and said, "You know, I just told them that when I taught, they had to listen, and I never taught them anything but the Bible."

Charles Evans Hughes testified it was because of that Sunday School teacher that God blessed him to have the success he had experienced.

Those who teach Sunday School classes need to be building solid. A teacher needs to be working well, for no one knows whose ears are hearing what is said, or whose eyes are seeing how one lives. Build upon the Book; discipline that class; and teach them the ways of God. If they don't like it, at least they will dislike something they should have liked. Teachers should stick to their ground and build quality into every child.

Some people are reaping the lack of quality in their lives today because of mistakes made thirty years ago. Life now

There's a great Christian layman in New Mexico whom I observed at a park one time with many little children. He had bought ice cream, cokes, and hot dogs for them. This man, who had no children of his own, was out there in the midst of those children.

Knowing he had paid for all of that, I said, "Those kids are really having fun, aren't they?" He said, "Yes, and *this* is the kid who is having the most fun."

It's good to invest in a life! To do something good and right and unselfish and Christ-like is not to lose, but to gain. The reward will take care of itself. The reward is a job well-done for Jesus' sake.

GIVE THE BEST COMFORT POSSIBLE

To do a job well, and to build solid, is to give the best comfort possible to the Lord Jesus Christ. When Jesus came to Jacob's well, he made practical use of it. He sat down, rested on the curb, and asked for a drink of water. Also, he began to talk to the woman about the water of life and the spirituality of true worship. He even revealed to her that he was indeed the Messiah.

To work well is to bring a blessing ultimately to God and to others. Hebrews 12:1-2 stresses that we have a whole arena of witnesses watching. When we do a shortcut in God's work, somebody in heaven knows it. First Timothy teaches that even the angels are observing our work. Mark 4 says that if we give a cup of water in the name of Jesus, we have a reward. Matthew 25:40 tells us, " . . . Inasmuch as ye have done it unto one of the least of these my brethren, ye have done it unto me." The Bible related that when Jacob came to the time of his death, he did not refer to this well that he had built with such quality. The Bible says that Jacob lay on his death bed thinking back ninety-seven years earlier where he had committed his life to God at Bethel.

Then Jacob rested, for he knew that he had done a good

job with that well. He recognized he had done a good job with everything since ninety-seven years ago, because ninety-seven years ago he had committed his all to God.

God puts no premium on ignorance or laziness. God wants us to be the best we can be in everything we can. We must work and build solid, especially as we invest in the lives of others.

9
A New Commitment to an Ancient Commission

Presidential Address
Baptist General Convention of Oklahoma
November, 1980

It has been said of the church, and most critically, I might add:

> Outwardly splendid as of old;/inwardly sparkless, void and cold;/her force and fire all spent and gone;/like the dead moon, she still shines on.

The church of the Lord Jesus Christ is not simply a reflection of greater days of dedication in the past. It is not a cut flower with a little bit of beauty for a moment, but soon to lose its fragrance because it has lost its power and dedication. I believe the greatest days of the church of the Lord Jesus Christ are ahead of us. However, that is only going to be true when *we* have a new and greater loyalty—a new commitment to an ancient commission.

Let's examine Matthew 28:16-20:

> Then the eleven disciples went away into Galilee, into a mountain where Jesus had appointed them. And when they saw him, they worshipped him: but some doubted. And Jesus came and spake unto them, saying, All power is given unto me in heaven

and in earth. Go ye therefore, and teach all nations, baptizing them in the name of the Father, and of the Son, and of the Holy Ghost: Teaching them to observe all things whatsoever I have commanded you: and, lo, I am with you alway, even unto the end of the world.

Let us see a new commitment to an ancient commission in five thoughts.

IT IS POINTED IN ITS COMMAND

The small, but very powerful, word *go* is most important. The word *go* is not a general suggestion like a cafeteria choice. It is not a sterile implication. It is as pointed as an Apache arrow, piercing the complacency of lethargic hearts. "GO!" the lord commanded clearly and unmistakably.

Now, there are those who preach this passage and claim that we can go through our thoughts. We can go through prayer. We can go through giving. Of course, all of us know there are those who cannot physically be out of the house, but when the Bible declares "Go" it is a pointed command. It gives no room for variation.

Imagine a general leading his men into battle. As they are ready to go forward, he announces "Onward, men! Now, some of you will go onward by staying, and some of you will go onward by eating, and some of you will go onward by remaining in your tents." If we spiritualize and play loose with what Jesus Christ has commanded, we will lose the genuine spirit of his command. The word GO is the word **go.** You do not *go* through praying; you pray through praying. You do not *go* through giving; you give through giving. You only GO when you GO! You must be willing to move out. There is no room for an elastic stretching of interpretation. We should not use *eisegesis* (putting thoughts into the text) in interpreting this passage, but it must be correctly *exegeted* (gaining thoughts

out of the text). The exposition of it is the fact that Jesus gave that pointed word: GO.

The real difference between religion and Christianity is this word "go." Herein lies the difference! Religion is man's insatiable desire to discover God. That's why Indians built totem poles. That's why there are hieroglyphics in the pyramids and sign-language paintings inside of caves. Man is searching for God. But Christianity is God coming down in flesh—we call the word "incarnation." "Carne" means flesh—God came in the "flesh." Everything God was and is Jesus was and is. He came and lived and walked upon this earth as God incarnate.

Religion is groping in the darkness of the philosophies of men, trying somehow to discover deity, while all the time God in Christianity comes to mankind. It is the nature of Christianity that man not seek God, but God has sought men in the person of Jesus Christ. Consequently, it must be the nature of those who follow Christ to seek other men. That is the precise nature of our Christianity. That is why that succinct, but powerful, word *"go"* is so essential to understanding what it's all about. We are to go. We are not cloistered monks in sanctuaries of self-righteousness. We do not create sacred societies for the snubbing of sinners. We are soldiers who go.

We are to go out into the world where there are sinners—out in the dives and the pits. Whether a man is lodging in the lap of luxury or bowing under the weight of poverty, his need is still the same. He needs someone to approach him with the pure gospel of Jesus Christ. It is pointed in its command. When the Holy Spirit came to Philip in Acts 8, the Spirit said, GO.

Someone asked a little boy about his old horse. "Son, can he run fast?" The boy answered, "No, sir, but he can stand fast." Have you ever known Baptists who couldn't move, but who could really stand? They could stand fast that was about it. A lot of people's favorite song is "Take My Life and Let It Be." My brother-in-law, Tom Elliff, has an excellent interpre-

tation of this idea. His theory is this: when many people walk the aisle of their church, are handed cards to fill out, and are then told to "be seated," they think they have just been given the Great Commission! However, they've only heard the words, "be seated." Man, they do a wonderful job of that!

Religion is not the hope of man. It is something more than that. Nicodemus was religious but lost. Lydia was religious but lost. The rich young ruler was religious but lost. Judas was religious but lost. What people need is someone to come to them with the claims of Jesus Christ.

IT IS PERSONAL IN ITS CALL

Here the word "ye" is a very original Greek construction. "Go" would have been adequate and should have been sufficient. After all, those to whom Jesus was speaking knew he wasn't speaking to trees. But he said, "Ye!" Why did he add "you" (or "ye")? Simple. He did it in case some people might have thought he didn't mean them.

You, pastor, who gets so terrestially tired that you don't celestially care. You, music director, who may sometimes be tempted to substitute talent for testimony and performance for purpose. You, deacon, who may often be more interested in hearing a financial report than someone praying, "Lord, be merciful to me, a sinner." YOU! You, chairman of the finance committee, who loves to be in a negative mood all the time. You, who sing in the choir. We have no talent; we have no money; we have no attributes. No! There is no excuse that is acceptable to God for refusing to go out into the world. Preachers must go. Singers must go. WMU ladies must go. Brotherhood men must go. Millionaires must go. We are all to GO! Even those who say it's not their gift.

My dad used to tell me, "Son, take out the garbage." If I had said, "Dad, that's not my gift," he would have given me a look that would have made me answer, "Dad, I just got the gift!" We do not go because it is a gift. We go because we love

A NEW COMMITMENT TO AN ANCIENT COMMISSION

Jesus. We GO because it is in our hearts.

I am often on the road, but when I am almost home, I start thinking about how nice it will be to walk in and see my beautiful wife. I know she is going to welcome me with a kiss. I don't sit in the car and think, *Oh, no! I've got to go into the house. My wife is going to kiss me.* The truth is, I can't wait to get home. I love that woman. What you and I need is such a love for the Lord Jesus Christ that we don't have to be propped up—we don't have to be promoted—we don't have to be prompted. We ought to be so excited about Jesus that we don't ever ask, "Do I have to witness?" We should be willing to say, "Give me a prospect! I'll go get him!" When our love for Jesus is like our love should be, it is the natural result of our testimony that we share the gospel of Jesus Christ.

Matthew 28:17 says: ". . . but some doubted." Commentary after commentary the writers indicate, "Some of the disciples did not believe in Jesus, even after this long forty-day period in which he was indeed resurrected." They doubted. Some say, "Well, what if I don't believe. Should I still go?" We've got to go. We've got to witness. Do you know why Jesus said to the skeptics, "Go"? Do you know why he said to the doubters, "Go"? Because nothing on this earth warms the heart of a doubter more than sharing the gospel of Christ and seeing a person born into the kingdom of God. This world needs someone like *you* to go.

We don't know, of course, how many were there when Jesus gave the Commission. Many think eleven. Paul wrote in 1 Corinthians 15:6, as he related this event, that there were "above five hundred." This is the commonly accepted view. So, some doubters probably were present, but he said to the doubters as well, "I want you to go."

Daddy Buckner is one of my favorite men to read about. He started what we used to call an "Orphans' Home." Now we call it a "Children's Home" on Samuel Boulevard in East Dallas. What a great Baptist pioneer he was! He loved little

children. They seem to be magnetized to him. As Daddy Buckner came into that place one day, a little girl had just entered the home. Her mother and father had been burned to death, along with three of her brothers and sisters. She was the only one left. Her name was Mary, and one side of her face was terribly scarred. The old red skin had grown taut, and it was hideously unattractive. When Mary came into the orphanage that day, Daddy Buckner was there, and children were all around him. Finally, when all the children were scattered, little Mary came and hugged the big man around his knees. She put her head on his trouser leg and said, "Daddy Buckner, you're gonna have to be my mommy and daddy both." He answered, "Mary, I'll try. I'll do my best."

Daddy Buckner was preaching one day, and when he came in, all the little children flocked around. He often gave them candy. He looked over and saw that Mary wasn't there around his feet as the other children were. She was over in a corner sobbing, and her shoulders were shaking. Finally, he told the other children to run and play, and he went over to her. When Mary saw him coming, she ran to him. He picked her up in his arms and asked, "Mary, what's wrong with you?" She replied, "Oh, Daddy Buckner, I know my face is ugly, and I know I'm ugly. Daddy Buckner, would you just kiss me on the cheek of my good side and tell me you love me?" That man began to kiss her all over her face and said, "Mary, those scars aren't ugly. They're beautiful. I love you, Mary."

This is an ugly world. Its sins are repulsive. Its sins are easy to hate, and some people in this world have some evil denials in areas of morality and purity. Even though they may be scarred, we must love them in the name of Jesus. The Great Commission is not only pointed in its command—it is personal in its call.

IT IS ALSO POWERFUL IN ITS COMPANIONSHIP

Have you ever noticed the word *therefore?* It is the third word in the Great Commission. "Go ye therefore...."

A NEW COMMITMENT TO AN ANCIENT COMMISSION

When a "therefore" appears, one needs to see what it is "there for." Why did he say *therefore*? To what did *therefore* point? It pointed to the fact that he had just reassured them, "All power is given unto me in heaven and in earth." Without that reality, we would be lonely Christians.

One man was trying to cure his loneliness and sent his picture to a lonely hearts club. They sent it back with the notation, "We are not that lonely." All kidding aside, it is a lonely world without Jesus Christ. Can you believe that our Companion, according to the Bible, has all power? "All power" means two things. First, it means there is no power that he does not have. Second, no one else has His power. He is the possessor of all the power.

Some say, "Oh, now, wait a minute. The devil has power." True, but only that which God will let him have. Jesus declared, "I have *all* power." He means just that. Satan had two big weapons. One was sin, and the other death. Satan said, "I believe with sin I can make men so evil and so rotten that Christ can never get them back." But Jesus said to those disciples, "I want you to go. You will have all power because I have all power, and I will literally pour my power into you." That's why he promised in John 14:6, as he was leaving, "You will be able to do greater things than I have done." He meant that he was leaving the Holy Spirit who would indwell all Christians everywhere.

Even though he was physically gone, He did something even better than raising Lazarus from the dead, better than walking on water, better than turning the water into wine, better than making the lame walk, better than making the blind see. He left the power enabling a Christian to tell people, through the power of the Holy Spirit, that they can be born into the kingdom of God. Jesus said, "I give you all power." It is powerful in its companionship.

But what about sin? The devil said, "I'll do these Christians in." S. D. Gordon, one of the greatest devotional preachers of all time was once out walking, and a little boy had a cage of

four birds. He asked the little boy, "Son, what are you going to do with those birds?" The boy said, "Oh, sir, I'll tell you what I am going to do. I am going to play with them awhile—then give them to my cat." Gordon said, "Little boy, let me buy those birds." The boy replied, "Oh, no, preacher, I couldn't sell you these birds. They are just field birds. Go get your own." S. D. Gordon said, "Son, I'd love to have those very birds. Could I buy them? What do you want for them?" The boy contended, "No, they are not for sale. You cannot buy them." Gordon said, "I'll give you two dollars for your cage and two dollars for your birds." The little boy thought awhile—then he sold those birds to Mr. Gordon.

Gordon then took the cage of birds. He thought they looked as though they had known they were going to their deaths. He took them over to a field, opened the little door of the cage so they could get out. However, they wouldn't go out. Finally, he tipped it over a little bit and tapped the cage. At last, one by one their wings unfolded, and all the little birds left. He said it seemed as though the birds were singing one song in unison, "Set free! Set free!"

It reminded Gordon of an old story about when old Lucifer saw that his hellish forces had men and women and boys and girls by the napes of their necks, and he put them in a cage. Along came Jesus and saw the people. Satan said, "You cannot have the souls of these people." Jesus replied, "Satan, I want to buy them." Satan said, "I've got all the gold I need. I won't sell the souls of men for gold or for silver or for religion or for works of righteousness." Jesus said to Lucifer, "I was not thinking of gold and silver or works of righteousness. I was thinking about giving my blood for those you have taken prisoner." When Lucifer heard that, he answered, "It's a deal!" And Jesus took that cage full of sinners who were locked up in the evil of the world—in the very throes of hell. Then, he shed his blood, and when he did, the door of the cage of sin flew open, and out the people came. *Free* from now throughout all

A NEW COMMITMENT TO AN ANCIENT COMMISSION

eternity. Oh, the chorus! One harmonious song, "Redeemed, redeemed, redeemed." We have been redeemed. Satan, who thought he could rob Christ of His power, had no strength to take the power of Christ.

There was another threat of Satan. It was called death. When Satan saw that sin could not bring about the final curse, he chuckled, "Death will do it. I will kill man, and I will kill Jesus." What Satan did not know at that time was that when Jesus died, Satan became the real loser. He became a defeated foe. And now, his time is numbered. Aren't you glad that because Jesus died, death died. *Death is dead.* We don't have to fear it. We can laugh in the face of death.

A little girl was dying of leukemia, and her mother leaned over her bed. The mother was crying, the girl noticed, and said, "Mother, don't cry."

The mother said, "Honey, I just have to cry some." That frail, pale girl tried to comfort her weeping mother, "Mother, do you remember the picnic?"

"Honey, please don't talk about things like that at this time. What do you mean about the picnic?"

"Mother, don't you remember the picnic? As we were out that day, a bee came along and stung you on the arm, and you said 'ouch!' and then it flew around a little bit more and came and lit on me. When I jumped, you said, 'Don't worry about that bee because a bee can only sting one person. It left its stinger in me.'

"Mother, don't you know that one time Death was flying around, and it stung Jesus and left its stinger in him. Mother, don't you cry. Death can't sting me today."

First Corinthians 15:56-57 tells us, "The sting of death is sin; and the strength of sin is the law. But thanks be to God, which giveth us the victory through our Lord Jesus Christ." We have the victory through Jesus Christ our Lord. I'm telling you, he has *all* power. And not even hell or sin or death can steal it from him.

It is not only pointed in its command, personal in its call, powerful in its companionship, but it is also precise in its cause.

IT IS PRECISE IN ITS CAUSE

When I say "cause," I am not thinking in terms of "because" or "causative force." I am speaking of cause in the sense one would think about the cause of freedom or the cause of Christ or the cause of righteousness or the cause of holiness. Jesus says that when we go, we are to go in the name of the Father and of the Son and of the Holy Spirit. We are not to be pale, placid politicians, compromising our commission. We are not to be ambassadors of benign beatitudes. We are to be proclaimers of the old-time, all-the-time, anytime, new-time glorious gospel of Jesus Christ. It is not a generalized effort—it is a precise cause.

How are we to go? As public relations officers for all the world? No! We are to go as ambassadors of *the* Father, and of *the* Son, and of *the* Holy Spirit, teaching them, as he said, "whatsoever I have commanded you."

If we want a new commitment to this ancient commission, two things must happen. First, there must be a new, bold declaration of respect for the Bible. There are those who say, "We've got to quit worrying about the Bible, and get busy about evangelism and missions." No sane soldier ever wanted to go into battle with a defective weapon. Imagine sailors on a ship trying to fire those big guns from that vessel and someone saying, "Sir, we've got a big hole in the ship, and we are sinking." Would the captain say, "Forget the sinking, and keep firing!"?

If the Bible is full of fables, folklore, fairy tales, myths, and mistakes, we are on a sinking ship. The Bible is the inerrant, infallible Word of God. All of it! And, as we preach it, we learn that the issues of our faith are centered in what people think of the Word of God.

A NEW COMMITMENT TO AN ANCIENT COMMISSION

Second, there must be a real understanding of what hell is all about. Someone said to William Booth, the founder of the Salvation Army, "Is it true that your training is the best training to win people to Christ?" He said, "No!" They replied, "But we understood that it was." Booth answered "The best training would be to spend five seconds in hell." If we could only see how lost man truly is!

We must also be committed to Bold Mission Thrust. However, it will never be Bold Mission Thrust unless it means that we have a bold declaration about the person of Christ. Our mission is the souls of men, and our thrust is empowered by the Holy Spirit. When we do that, Bold Mission Thrust will become a reality.

The Great Commission is also . . .

PRECIOUS IN ITS CONSUMMATION

A. T. Robertson comments on this last phrase, "even unto the end of the world." He related that this does not mean to the end of the earth, but to the consummation of the age, at which time the Son of God shall appear in glory. One precious thought about the Great Commission is that we are never alone. He is with us now until the glorious day when he shall appear.

After the Ayatollah Khomeini lived all those years in France, he returned to Tehran in a 747 airplane. They circled the Tehran airport, and all of the Iranians looked up at Khomeini and cried, "Our savior, our savior, our savior." I want you to know that one day our real Savior is coming, but it will not be in a 747, because He is 777. (By the way, he is going to clobber 666!) Oh, the consummation of the ages! He said, "Lo, I will be with you until the consummation of the age." It is precious. It gets better and better all the way.

It is precious in its consummation.

Reginald Heber wrote "From Greenland's Icy Mountains." In the third verse he penned:

Shall we whose souls are lighted with wisdom from on high, shall we to men benighted the Lamp of life deny? Salvation, Oh Salvation, the joyful sound proclaim till Earth's remotest nation has learned Messiah's name.

10
Characteristics of a Dynamic Church

It is very obvious that we have tremendous needs in our churches. On the whole, we are not experiencing church growth like we used to, and it is a serious failing.

Sunday School was once the charm of the Southern Baptist Convention. It was, in J. N. Barnette's words, *The Pull of the People.* In one recent year, there was a net loss in SBC Sunday School enrollment of 100,000 people. Ninety percent of the prospects for your church are twenty-one years and older. It is a day where we should put a tremendous emphasis on reaching adults for Christ. For every existing church in America there are 4,000 adult prospects available to be reached.

Dr. Bill Hogue, once reported that we had gone down in baptisms three years consecutively. (Thank God the trend is being reversed.) Then he made a harsh and alarming statement. "That is the prelude to the decline of our denomination." That was sad to hear, and something you would expect a denominational rebel to say—not a denominational servant. We are going the way of other mainline denominations because of this almost perpetual decline in church growth and baptisms.

A climate for church growth is obviously a relevant subject for the situation in which Southern Baptists and others find themselves. There is a pressing need for church growth. In

one recent year Southern Baptist churches had no baptisms. I was in a certain state for an evangelism conference, and they announced that out of 866 churches (most of them with a full-time pastor) in the state, 436 of them did not baptize one person!

Apparently, we have heard what we have been taught lately. We have heard criticisms of bus ministry, of evangelists, of numbers, and—sure enough—we have received the mistaken idea that we don't need numbers or a bus ministry or an emphasis on setting goals. Finally, what we have either heard by direct remark or innuendo has gotten through to us! And what is that? That we don't have to reach people. It is sad how this has been communicated, but it's happened. That ill-conceived notion has lured many of our churches into lethargy.

Let's examine ten elements we can apply in churches that will create church growth.

A GROWING CHURCH NEEDS TO HAVE A JOYFUL CLIMATE

Every church that grows is a church which has joy and excitement. The biblical admonition in Phillipians 4:4 is true, "Rejoice in the Lord alway: and again I say, Rejoice." There is not as much joy as there ought to be. This is true even in the home.

One husband looked at his wife after she displeased him and carped, "Honey, how could the Lord make you so beautiful but so cotton-pickin' dumb?" She retorted, "I guess the Lord made me beautiful so *you* could love me, and made me dumb so *I* could love you."

Lack of compatibility is often a severe problem, whether it is in the government, in labor, in management, in the home, or the church. It is always sad to hear someone say about a church, "They are having problems." That is sad. It should not be. There should be rejoicing in every church. "A merry heart doeth good like a medicine," the Scriptures teach, and a

CHARACTERISTICS OF A DYNAMIC CHURCH

church ought to be of medicinal value for every one who comes. The Balm of Gilead should be applied to every social, spiritual, and emotional wound of those who enter the doors of our churches.

It might be a good idea to move the pulpit from the inside of the church to the outside of the church. Probably a good place for the sermon to be preached is from the steps of the church, not from the interior—the reason being the many things that should be done before we even enter the church. There should be cleansing and a new sense of forgiveness. There should be a sense of joy and a spirit of rejoicing. The pulpit should be moved to the front steps of the church and the preacher should say, *"Before* you enter, you need to make some decisions. *Before* we can even start to worship God, there needs to be a spirit of joy."

Sometime ago I was at one of our great churches, and the joy of that church was something to behold. They were running close to 3,000 in Sunday School and well over that in church services. They were rejoicing and full of happiness.

At one of our Starlite Crusades in Del City a musical group was playing. I couldn't help but notice a lady about seventy years of age sitting there while the group was singing "Gospel Ship." It was a very upbeat song, with plenty of rhythm and excitement. The lady had both feet going up and down. She was tapping her feet and really "gettin' with it." I noticed that her hose had fallen down around her ankles. They looked like two, big nylon doughnuts and I became tickled. It was almost hilarious. She was really enjoying that revival meeting. Now, I realize it's not essential to have your hose drop to your ankles to "get with it," but she was excited.

One night our church soloist caught me totally off guard. As I came to the pulpit, she asked me to sing a duet with her. Friends, I am probably the world's lousiest singer! A few years ago at my father-in-law's home, while we were all going into the living room to sing Christmas carols, my brother-in-law

said, "Bailey, if you will go outside and play with the dog, we'll be through in just a few minutes." That's the kind of voice I have. But, I received a standing ovation for singing that duet in our church. Oh, how there needs to be that joy and freedom of expression in every church.

A GROWING CHURCH NEEDS TO HAVE A LOVING CLIMATE

There needs to be love and acceptance. God has given the world the right to judge us by how we love one another. The Bible teaches that they shall know we are his disciples by our love for each other. A loving and forgiving relationship—not judgmental—one that understands. The church is a place where no grudges are allowed. The only person who can afford not to forgive is the person who has never been in need of forgiveness.

Where there is that kind of acceptance, love, and joy, there will be a growing church. People want to be part of something that is happening and something that is loving.

Recently, while in an evangelism conference, I met a man who prayed a prayer that in some measure changed my life. He prayed, "Dear God, I want to thank you that two years ago a Christian couple didn't see a Mexican, but they saw a person who needed Jesus Christ."

After the service I talked with the man, and he said, "Yes, that couple led me to the Lord." The Lord put a phrase in my mind that has been a real source of joy to me. "There is only one kind of person in the world, and that is a person for whom Jesus died." There are no rich people, poor people, illiterate people, educated people, red people, black people, or white people, yellow or brown people—there is only one kind of person and that is the kind of person for whom Jesus died.

Our churches need to be loving. Regardless of race or social standing, when a person comes to our church, they should be made to feel welcome. We need a loving relationship.

A GROWING CHURCH NEEDS A BIBLE-CENTERED CLIMATE

A magazine reported sometime ago that churches were failing. One former pastor wrote an article about why churches were failing. It is amazing to me that when a man messes up his church, he can tell you how to run yours.

This fellow had lost his church, and he began to list the things not to do. He had decided that they no longer needed gospel preaching and singing—they needed to do drama to interpret the Bible. So all the staff came out on Sunday morning in leotards and did a little interpretation of some great Scripture passage and pretty soon nobody came.

It's my conviction that any church which goes out of business ought to. I don't know of any Bible-believing, Bible-preaching church that has had to close its doors. A church once had a striptease act under the guise of ministry. I understand that church is now having tremendous problems. Praise God—it ought to go out of business if that's its ministry.

A church which is Bible-centered is a church that grows and creates a climate for growth. When you think of the largest churches in the Southern Baptist Convention, you will find Bible-believing pastors. The Bible says that we are earthen vessels, not designed to preach ourselves, but Jesus Christ and him only. A man who preaches himself has a church as big as he is. But a man who preaches the Bible has a church as big as God. We need Bible-centered churches.

A GROWING CHURCH MUST HAVE A CLIMATE OF ENTHUSIASM

The word enthusiasm comes from the Greek words "en" and "Theos" which together literally mean to be "in God." In a real sense, the Rotarians, the Lions, or the Chamber of Commerce cannot have enthusiasm. Only the church of Jesus Christ can know true enthusiasm, according to its definition.

When one is filled with God, it is like an ever-present artes-

ian well bubbling over in Him. Enthusiasm for a child of God is not something that he has worked up. It is something that God has sent down. It is something in his heart. If you find an enthusiastic church, you will find an enthusiastic preacher.

A preacher friend of mine was recently witnessing to an agnostic. This man was very critical, fault-finding and skeptical. Later, I talked with the former agnostic. He had come to know Christ and was then an excited Christian. He said, "I want to tell you something, Bailey. When I heard that preacher preach, I did not believe one thing he preached, but I was totally convinced that *he* believed it. When I was convinced of that, it made me want to inquire about that man, about his beliefs, and that is the way I came to know Christ."

There was a preacher who couldn't understand why people were going to sleep during his sermons, so he recorded a few sermons to see what was wrong. As he was listening to the tapes, he went to sleep! That's the truth! Lack of enthusiasm is really inexcusable in church. We need enthusiastic preachers in order to have enthusiastic churches.

The preaching should not only be enthusiastic, but the services should be likewise. The music needs to be alive! A church can't have Baptist preaching and formal music! That won't "hack it." There has to be something that is alive!

Too many musicians love music more than they love Jesus. If our desire is to please the music faculty at some music school, then we can please the musicians. But if our desire is to reach people for Jesus, we must please our Father in heaven. There is all the difference in the world.

Sometimes our sermons would get an "A" in homiletics class, but no converts. Sometimes our music would be great for a recital, but it means nothing to the kingdom of God. Church services must be result-centered and result-conscious.

Music needs to be worshipful, yet exciting, in order to reach people. Churches need to be excited and enthusiastic.

A GROWING CHURCH NEEDS A CLIMATE OF FREEDOM

There needs to be a relaxed atmosphere. When I first came to First Southern Baptist of Del City, I noticed a lot of laughter going on before services. It sounded like a beehive. I thought, *Oh, no. What is this? People are talking, chattering, and running every place.* My first thought was that I wanted to make this service worshipful. I remember thinking, *How am I going to stop this racket and chattering?* Then the answer came to me, "Smith, if you stop it, you will kill the church's enthusiasm."

Many churches aren't worried about noise. It takes people to make noise. Churches all over our denomination are dying because of something called "worship" (more clearly, "liturgy"). The reason people were laughing, talking, and chattering was they were glad to see one another. And I said, "Bailey Smith, you cannot kill that in this church." It is better to have laughter with people than *no* people. There needs to be that freedom.

A GROWING CHURCH NEEDS TO BE EVANGELISTIC

How is a church evangelistic? In the first place, it must have an evangelistic pastor.

In a revival sometime ago a very sad thing happened to me. I was in a car with a friend and he knew he could say anything to me that he needed to say. We were backing out of the parking lot and that man said to me, "Oh, I wish our pastor would give us an example." Folks, that disturbed me when he said that.

In Acts 4 Peter and John were going to the Temple, and a lame man looked up. He was asking alms, but Peter and John said, "Silver and gold have I none, but such as I have give I

thee in the name of Jesus. Rise up and walk." And the man was healed. It is interesting that the man asked for a penny, but he got new legs. Which do you think he really preferred—the penny or the new legs? The answer is obvious. Why didn't he *ask* for new legs instead of alms? Because he didn't know he had a choice.

Our community does not say, "Tell us about hell. Tell us about heaven." Our communities will ask to be provided with recreation and to be socialized. What our communities really need is something they do not have enough spiritual insight to ask for—and that is the life-transforming power of Jesus Christ. This is the real need!

The poor man in Acts 4 actually wanted new legs, but he didn't ask for them because he didn't know he could have them. By the same token, our lost world is not aware of the miraculous power of Christ, but when they experience it, they find that is what they have been longing for all the time. The only thing that fills the void of an empty heart is the experience of Jesus Christ. Churches must be evangelistic.

A magazine called me sometime ago to see if they could interview me. The editor of the magazine talked with me for about an hour. After I told him some things about our church, he said, "Well, our church does that, but we still don't have the number of people saved that your church does. We still don't have that excitement you are talking about."

You see—the difference is the evangelism itself. What brings joy to people is seeing other people saved. What brings excitement to a church is seeing people born into the kingdom.

You can have gospel-preaching and Bible-believing people, and you can have the greatest organization, but unless people are saved, people go away without real joy and excitement. It is seeing people saved that creates joy and excitement.

A GROWING CHURCH NEEDS A CLIMATE OF AUTHORITY

Authority is not demanded so much as it is given. Some think it is to be earned. Yes, but it is also given. Authority has to be earned. People have to respect a man before he can be the leader of the church. If a pastor ever bucks his church, he had better make sure he is right. A church wants their pastor to lead, but he needs to be correct when he does.

There has to be a time when the church learns who the pastor is. There has to come that time. Now, it may be slower in some churches than in others, but pastoral authority must be recognized. Authority needs to be given. It is a sad situation when a man has to convince a church that he is the pastor.

Immediately after coming to Del City a matter came up in deacons' meeting about a staff member. I thought, *Oh, my, what's going to happen?* By the way, this was my first deacons' meeting. The chairman of the deacons said to the deacon talking about the staff member, "Wait a minute. We have a pastor and he is seated right over here. The staff does not work for the church—it works for the pastor. If the pastor likes what that staff member is doing, that's fine. If he doesn't, *he* can correct it." I sat there acting like that was the way I had always believed, but deep down I thought, *I didn't know that.* Many folks thought I was being wise because of my silence, but it was really fear. That is why I didn't burst in there and say something. Authority needs to be given.

The pastor must be the authority of the church. If the deacons run the church, it is not a Baptist church. The "presbytery" is the government of another kind of Church. "Boards of deacons" are foreign to the New Testament.

One pastor told me, "You know, I wanted our church to have a mission." He was so sad as he talked. "The church voted it down," he said. Most people would be amazed to find

that the top churches of our denomination will not turn down anything the pastor recommends. Why? The answer is that there is a fearful responsibility for pastoral authority because God has commissioned the pastor to be the shepherd and leader of that church.

A GROWING CHURCH MUST HAVE A DARING CLIMATE

C. T. Studd, a man of unbelievable spiritual power, said, "Some wish to live within the sound of church and chapel bell; but I want to run a rescue shop within a yard of hell." There must be a daring ministry.

In order for a preacher to build a church, he must think bigger than himself. As I look back at some of my early churches, I remember trying to build them around my opinions, my ideas, and my horizons. Then, I saw the smallness of Bailey Smith (and that is very small).

I remember praying at 2 o'clock one morning at a particular pastorate with a couple of other men. During this time, God said something to me that really shocked me. He said, "Bailey Smith, you don't have a ministry. You have a career." I found that God was exactly right, because I found myself protecting every thought about what I did. I wanted to make sure that the pulpit committee from "First Baptist Church, County Seat Town" found no black marks upon my leadership. I found that I had a career and not a ministry.

When the Lord revealed that to me for the first time, I really became willing to fail totally as a preacher. I was willing to do things that seemed to be ridiculous—things that I didn't like, things that my opinions and my bigotry would not allow me to do—but things I knew God wanted done. We started some unusual ministries, and all of a sudden the church changed. It doubled in size. It became a great evangelistic church.

If you build your church around you, it will be too small.

CHARACTERISTICS OF A DYNAMIC CHURCH

There are churches that have pony rides and all kinds of excitement going on, and my first attitude used to be critical, but now I'm not. Who says a church has to be dull and dry? My opinion really doesn't matter.

A lot of things that we do around the church don't especially appeal to me. Our minister of music spoke to one of the dignified ladies in our choir after she had complained about the fact that he had done some "country" gospel music. He replied, "I hate it, but it is not important that I fulfill my opinion. It is important that somebody is reached for Jesus."

The main thing that the pastor must overcome is his innate, personal inhibition against some things that will build his church.

Years ago two boys—now men—were converted at a revival meeting. Now, thousands of people have been converted because of their ministry. And yet, they came to church one evening for only one reason: a lady told them they would get some ice cream afterwards.

It matters not why people come to church, if they leave with Jesus! There needs to be a willingness to be daring and for every church to grow, there must be that climate.

A GROWING CHURCH MUST HAVE A CLIMATE OF FAITH

I asked a leading pastor why his church became great, and he said, "It got like it is because we had men in our church who were willing to believe God, willing to let the church spend some money, to launch out, to be obligated and to be challenged." The church must be a people of faith.

A little sign on my desk reads, "God never puts in the hearts of his people a dream unless he gives them the ability to fulfill it." I believe this is true. It is imperative that we be a people of faith.

To me the saddest story in the Bible is in Matthew 17. The disciples tried to cast demons out of a possessed boy, but they

couldn't. They complained, "Jesus, we tried to heal this boy, but why can't we do it?" Jesus said, "You couldn't do it because of your unbelief."

I wonder how many people remain lost throughout the world because of Christian's lack of faith. Some people remain emotionally, mentally, and physically crippled because of unbelief.

A GROWING CHURCH MUST HAVE A CLIMATE OF PRAYERFULNESS

A church stands tall when it is on its knees. The only way for Christian soldiers to win the spiritual warfare is to have the posture of fighting on their knees.

A pulpit committee looking for a pastor called an associational missionary in West Texas and said, "Recommend a man to us." Now, in West Texas they always had big, strong, wide-shouldered, rugged men, and the associational missionary said, "How big a preacher do you want?" The chairman of the pulpit committee gave a great answer. He said, "We really don't care how big he is, but we would like a pastor who, when he gets on his knees, will reach to heaven." That's a good-sized preacher!

A church that is prayful is going to grow. Until you and I can talk to people about God, we must first learn to talk to God about people. The church bathed in prayer will be a growing church!

11
Echoes
of Encouragement

Let's examine Exodus 15:23-27:

> And when they came to Marah, they could not drink of the waters of Marah, for they were bitter: therefore the name of it was called Marah. And the people murmured against Moses, saying, What shall we drink? And he cried unto the Lord; and the Lord shewed him a tree, which when he had cast into the waters, the waters were made sweet: there he made for them a statute and an ordinance, and there he proved them. And said, If thou wilt diligently hearken to the voice of the Lord thy God, and wilt do that which is right in his sight, and wilt give ear to his commandments, and keep all his statutes, I will put none of these diseases upon thee, which I have brought upon the Egyptians; for I am the Lord that healeth thee. And they came to Elim, where were twelve wells of water and threescore and ten palm trees; and they encamped there by the waters.

Maybe you remember Naomi. She had her name changed to Marah because her life had been bitter. If there is one predominant word that would describe the feeling I find among pastors and church workers across America, it is the word *discouragement*. America needs to be encouraged.

I have to be careful when I preach because it is not encouraging to people for me to tell them what kind of people they really are. That sometimes is discouraging rather than encouraging. For this reason I am usually totally quiet about the good things that God has given in my own church.

I talked with an evangelist friend lately and asked him what he felt was the greatest need of people today. He said, "The greatest need is encouragement. People are so discouraged. In fact, if I were to count all of the happy pastors that I know of in the 200 churches that I was in last year, I could count only six that I would say are really happy."

Isn't that a shame? I know preachers get horribly criticized by their members sometimes. They get down and blue. One deacon recently said, "I have never seen my pastor's eyes shine. When he prays he closes his. When he preaches, I close mine." The pastor replied to this statement by saying, "When I am dead, shed no tears because I will be no deader then than you've been for years."

THE BATTLE IS THE LORD'S

Notice in this passage we find a grand and glorious word of encouragement. One titanic theme in this passage is the simple, yet profane, point: The battle is the Lord's. Forty-five times in eighteen verses of Exodus 15 we find this recurring theme. The battle is the Lord's.

While I lived in New Mexico I once tried to water the yard with a sprinkler that was about twelve years old. The sprinkler just barely moved around. As I was watching this sprinkler try to work, suddenly the sky darkened and there came the biggest rainstorm I had ever seen. As I sat there watching that sprinkler trying to work while the rains were falling, the Lord spoke to me. He said, "Do you see that old dilapidated water sprinkler? It looks like you appear in my perspective. The sprinkler is just barely going around. It's doing a mediocre job. And I, God, am doing much better at what that sprinkler is supposed to be doing."

I had to learn a long time ago that as a preacher or music director or educational director or associate pastor that we find ourselves hitching up our little mechanisms to get the work of God going, when what we really need to do is get down on our knees and pray for a blessing so that heaven might fall and God might bring refreshment to the land. How stupendous is the power that comes when we pray and submit to Him! He will do more than we ever thought we could do. You see, it's those people we get down the aisle that we see go out the other aisle. It's only what God does that lasts. That's the important thing.

All my life I was irritated by the people who kept saying, "It's not our ability; it's our availability." I got so tired of that. But I discovered that they were exactly right.

I know of several preachers who have tried to change their entire method of preaching. They have tried to be more like some of the big television evangelists, but their churches haven't grown. You see, it isn't the method that gets it done—it's the man. It's the power of God that's in a man submitted to God. What you and I need to understand is that the battle is the Lord's.

For me to be better for you, and for you to be better for me, and for us to be better for the Lord, is not to have a thousand seminars, but to have one moment when we get on our knees and say, "God, I belong to you." The power is the Lord's.

We have a week of prayer for Lottie Moon and Annie Armstrong, our denomination's special foreign and home missions appeals. We need a week of prayer for our individual churches. We need to get on our knees and say, "God, I submit myself wholly and totally unto you." The battle is the Lord's.

One of the greatest preachers in America is a black preacher from the North. I once heard him talk about the time his grandmother heard the Ku Klux Klan horsemen outside. They came in and got one of her sons out of the house. He

said they broke down his grandmother's door. They grabbed this seventeen-year-old boy and dragged him behind a horse down the street, hanged him up, and shot him full of holes. Then they dragged him back, opened the front door, threw his bleeding body into the house, and apologized to her by saying they had gotten the wrong guy. That dear, old grandmother picked up that son of hers and held that boy as he died in her arms.

The next morning, the same black woman got up to go to work. She went to the white plantation house and bathed little white children. She cooked for a white family. It never entered her mind to put poison in their food. It never entered her mind to take the butcher knife and plunge it into the heart of one of those little white boys out of revenge for that son whom white men had killed.

When she came home, this preacher's father said, "Mother, how could you go to the white man's house, wash and iron his clothes, cook his food, and bathe his children when they killed your boy?" She answered, "Because of the Lord's Prayer. 'Our Father which art in heaven, hallowed be thy name. Thy kingdom come . . . .' I must forgive. Vengeance is mine, saith the Lord. As I am to forgive my debtors, God will forgive me. I don't have to get back. God will measure it out some day." The battle is the Lord's. Oh, what encouragement!

Some need to change direction. The battle *is* the Lord's. Some are trying to overcome faults. Some are having terrible storms today because of yesterday's dark clouds.

After my son was born, I would come home and my wife would say, "You know, he's crawling today." Then he started toddling a little bit. But mostly, he fell. I began to think about it. When I came home his mother never reported his falls. When I walked in the door she never said, "Bailey, guess what. Scott fell 386 times today." Instead she would say, "Scott took two steps."

ECHOES OF ENCOURAGEMENT

My friend, God counts our steps, not our falls. Aren't we glad for a God like that?

REJOICING BELONGS TO THE REDEEMED

Rejoicing belongs to the redeemed. Look at verse 18: "The Lord shall reign for ever and ever." Look at them shouting that song. Then notice verses 20 and 21, "And Miriam the prophetess, the sister of Aaron, took a timbrel in her hand; and all the women went out after her with timbrels and with dances. And Miriam answered them, Sing ye to the Lord, for he hath triumphed gloriously; the horse and his rider hath he thrown into the sea."

They rejoiced and they began to be excited in the things of the Lord. The key to rejoicing is being saved. The next key to rejoicing is rejoicing. When you don't feel like praising the Lord, you should praise the Lord anyway. We are not made joyful by our circumstances. We are made happy by what is in us. The reason the Apostle Paul could say, "I have decided in whatever state I am in to be content," is because he had something in him more powerful than that which was outside him. Rejoicing belongs to the redeemed.

The happiest, most joyful, excited people on earth ought to be Christian people. When we begin to fuss at a little problem, all of a sudden we have created a big problem. Be careful. There is more rejoicing in heaven over one sinner who repents than ninety-nine who need no repentance.

While in Tennessee recently I was lent an automobile, and I drove out where the Grand Ole Opry is located. I came in the back way and was able to get near where the celebrities enter because I was on the program. I went in the back door and looked over and saw a security guard. He asked my name. I had arrived about thirty minutes early. That security guard looked a bit distressed, and I asked, "Sir, how are you doing?" He said, "Preacher, no one ever asked me that. I'm doing pretty good, but I have leukemia. It's the kind that gets in your

lymph glands. They are all over my body, and I probably don't have long to live.

I asked him, "If that leukemia gets you, what's going to happen to you?" Tears came to his eyes and he said, "I bet you want to know if I'm saved, don't you?" I said, "I probably would have gotten around to that." He said, "I'm not." I began to talk with him and it wasn't long before I said, "If I stretched across this counter and stuck out my hand, would you put your hand in it as a symbol that you want Jesus Christ as Savior? Would you invite Jesus into your heart?" He said, "I sure would, Preacher."

At that moment, the security guard invited Christ into his heart. After he finished praying, he said something to me that no one has ever said to me before after a soul-winning experience. He said, "Thank you for your courtesy." I just couldn't believe he said that, but I'll tell you one thing—it is a courteous thing to want people to go to heaven.

I was so jubilant. It is a rejoicing time. The most joyful people on earth are pure, whole, separated Christians who have given their lives fully to the Lord Jesus Christ. In this passage, they were rejoicing and shouting. They had the timbrels. Some of them were dancing and having a glorious time. Christians should be a happy people.

THERE ARE BLESSINGS IN BURDENS

There are blessings in burdens. Here were the children drinking the bitter waters of Marah. Notice verses 24 and 25, "And the people murmured against Moses, saying, What shall we drink? And he cried unto the Lord; and the Lord shewed him a tree, which when he had cast into the waters, the waters were made sweet; there he made for them a statute and an ordinance, and there he proved them."

Sometimes God gives us what we ask for before we need it in order to show us that we really didn't need what we asked for. We will soon see that point unfolding.

Then again, sometimes blessings can be poisonous. They

begged for water, but God knew it wasn't time for the miracle. Then they came to Marah and the very thing they asked God for was no good. They couldn't drink it.

Personally, I don't want anything before God wants me to have it. When we take of something before God is ready for us to have it, it will be a bitter thing. So, we find Israel at Marah asking, "Moses, what are we going to do?" Moses then turned to God and asked, "God, what are we going to do? What plan do you have?" God said, "Moses, if you will go cut down a tree and throw it into the water, the water will turn sweet."

One commentator said that when Moses threw the tree in, the leaves had a magnetism that got all of the incrustations out of the water, but I don't believe it really happened like that. This was undoubtedly a miracle of God.

I think the reason the tree was required is because the cross was made from a tree. That's why in 2 Peter 2:21 Peter said that He died on a tree for our sins.

When I look at a society that is wrecked and ruined, I know the cross needs to be thrown into those waters. When I see a home breaking up, I know it is the cross, the tree upon which Jesus died, that needs to be put into that home. When I see political corruption, I know the cross is the answer. Over and over again, the world should see that the tree needs to be put in the bitter waters that they might become sweet. Moses did what God said, and threw the tree into the water. The bitter water then became sweet. Sometimes you have to learn to wait for the sweetness.

WE CAN WATCH GOD'S MIRACLES

What an encouragement to us that even in the burdens of life we can watch the miracles of God. The fourth encouragement is that the best is yet to be. Look at verse 27, "And they came to Elim, where were twelve wells of water, and threescore and ten palm trees: and they encamped there by the waters."

There was a well for each tribe and a shade tree for each

elder. Elim is only ten miles from Marah. No matter how bad you think things are now, it's only ten more miles to Elim.

A missionary was given a poem that consisted of only two words:

> Go on, go on, go on;
> Go on, go on, go on;
> Go on, go on, go on.

Do you feel you are in Marah? Do you know how to get out of Marah? Go on, go on, go on. You can't stop at Marah. Go on. Elim is going to come.

A pastor friend of mine received a telephone call three days before Christmas from a strong, handsome sixteen-year-old wanting my friend's son to go hunting. Many things happened, but the conclusion of the story was that this dear friend accidentally put a bullet through the heart of that preacher's boy.

When I walked into their home recently, I saw a large portrait of that son. I asked the father how he could get over something like that. He said, "One doesn't. We will live all of our lives with a broken heart."

Then he said, "I want to show you something." We went down the hall to a bedroom, and he reached into a baby bed and pulled out a little baby girl. I said, "Where did you get her? I know your wife has not been pregnant." He replied, "A doctor in our church heard that we wanted a baby, and three days before Christmas—three years to the day after our son was killed—this doctor called to ask if we wanted a baby. We went down to that hospital. The mother never saw the baby. We'll never get over the loss of our boy, but look at what God has given us."

Marah is bitter, but Elim is just ten miles down the road. Don't despair. Don't give up. Go on, because tomorrow when you turn a corner, you will behold a ray of sunlight you never knew was there.

12
Let the Church Stand Up in Today's World

Keynote Message, SBC
June, 1976

The title of this chapter is very important. Let's begin by asking a most basic question. Is there a present need for the church to stand up in today's world? Is the above title no more than the result of a committee's frustration for theme material, or is it a whimsical roulette-wheel approach to selection, or a quick choice to meet the deadline for program planning? Is it a title for title's sake, or is it the expression of a viable issue?

Please allow me to answer my own question. When we live in a world where Christians and Muslims are warring against each other, and are making a rabble of a modern city, the church needs to stand up! When our world reads daily of pubs and bus stops and hotel rooms and men's rooms exploding from terrorist bombs because the Protestants and Catholics refuse to hear what they preach, the church must stand up.

Surrounded by the deterioration of basic principles and worthy institutions, realizing that eight percent of Americans attend church on Sunday morning, two percent on Sunday evening, and 61,000 churches reported no additions last year, I say, "let the church stand up." When our children go to schools where Genesis is made a hoax by the State-approved textbooks, and the intimacy between a man and woman is

portrayed in bathroom-wall language, the church must stand up!

When some men of the cloth are denying that the Bible is the Word of God and their churches are more amusement centers than houses of worship, let the church stand up! We have read of the number of churches which have bars, and we were sickened to read of the church in a certain state where a local stripper performed the full show for the Sunday morning parishioners in the sanctuary. There is also a church in another state that had baptismal services for the family pets.

The folly of that is well illustrated by the man who was told he would be employed at the department store if he would sell this one ugly green suit that had been there for time immemorial. In less than an hour, he sold it. The manager was amazed and said, "My, that is tremendous. You sold the suit no one has been able to sell. But where did you get all of those lacerations? Was the man who bought it angry?" "Oh, no, sir, but his seeing-eye dog almost killed me!" Dear friends, even a dog wouldn't buy some things going on in today's world.

Paul, encouraging the Ephesian church to stand up proudly and purely in the world, wrote in Ephesians 4:17-21;

> This I say therefore, and testify in the Lord, that ye henceforth walk not as other Gentiles walk, in the vanity of their mind, Having the understanding darkened, being alienated from the life of God through the ignorance that is in them, because of the blindness of their heart: Who being past feeling have given themselves over unto lasciviousness, to work all uncleanness with greediness. But ye have not so learned Christ; If so be that ye have heard him, and have been taught by him, as the truth is in Jesus.

My fellow Christians, the church is not like the world in blindness of heart and vanity of mind, but we have the truth in Jesus, and we must stand up and proclaim it.

THE CHURCH WILL STAND UP FOR GODLY STANDARDS IN TODAY'S WORLD

Paul says in verse 17, that we "walk not as other men," . . . "which is corrupt according to the deceitful lusts . . . " (as he mentions in verse 22)—because, as he continues in verse 25, we are " . . . putting away lying . . . for we are members one of another."

If there is a voice that cries out for unblemished purity, let it be God's church. If a word is spoken for integrity, honesty, and unmitigated ethics, let it be the virtuous bride of Christ. When it seems that the world is being engulfed by the darkness of filth and evil, let it be the might, thundering voice of the church that stands up and says there is a better way. And, if it seems that the world has, in apparent unanimous agreement, turned its back on the lonely, poor, and estranged, let it be the rising church that cries, "In the name of Jesus, friend of sinners, we love you."

Now, it is interesting that we can hear an apology made to the perverted, whose desires the Bible calls "unnatural affection," but for years we have been bombarded with four-letter words, jokes about unrestrained sex, scoffing about marriage and the home, God's name used in jest, the ministry of Jesus maligned, uncovered bodies displayed through our television screens, and no one takes even the briefest moment to apologize to us who find such things offensive. The church stands up in today's world with today's values and asserts, "You owe the good people of this world an apology."

Our country will forbid some churches from various religious practices because of the danger involved. And yet, alcohol, that has killed nearly 300,000 people within the last ten years, becomes the national pastime. The church stands up and says, "God's standard is higher than the bottle."

Philippians 4:8-9 says it well:

> Finally, brethren, whatsoever things are true, whatsoever things are honest, whatsoever things are

just, whatsoever things are pure, whatsoever things are lovely, whatsoever things are of good report; if there be any virtue, and if there be any praise, think on these things. Those things, which ye have both learned, and received, and heard, and seen in me, do: and the God of peace shall be with you.

THE CHURCH WILL STAND UP FOR DOMESTIC AND GLOBAL EVANGELISM IN TODAY'S WORLD

Paul says all through this majestic mountain peak of spiritual truth (in chapter four) that there is a vast difference between the Christian and the non-Christian. He tells us in verse 18 that ignorance is largely responsible. The lost must be told in order to have their blindness cured.

Our churches can honor the Father, whether we have a $100,000 organ or a clanging upright piano; whether we meet within chiseled stone or cement blocks; whether our pastor graduated from seminary or never made it there; whether the aisle is plush carpet or worn tile; whether we have a Bach anthem or a Gaither gospel; but it is impossible to honor the Father if our churches make evangelizing the lost and needy world secondary.

If we preach example, the Buddhist can produce Gautama, as their example. If we preach a teacher, Islam can produce Muhammad. If we preach patriotism, Shintoism can put us to shame. But nowhere in this world is there one who can be Savior other than he who graced Golgotha's crest. Man didn't need an example, a teacher, or a great patriot. He needed One who would die in his place and do death to his sin that through his death man might have everlasting life. Jesus died because there was a hell to escape—a heaven to gain—and if we get our churches involved with anything that slows evangelism, we have mocked the unique place of Christ in history as *Savior*.

One time a pastor friend and I were visiting. We went to

see a man that I knew only by reputation. I had counseled with his wife after he had beaten her severely several times. He had also neglected the children. His little daughter ran up to us that day as we approached the back door and said, "Daddy doesn't want you to come talk to him." We went on anyway.

We stood in the kitchen and talked because he wouldn't ask us into the living room. He cursed at us and made ugly remarks to his wife who was standing nearby. I got rather firm in my remarks—trying to break him loose. He turned red in the face and said, "I ought to shoot you." He reached over and grabbed the shotgun leaning in the corner. My brave evangelist jumped behind me. I grabbed the wrist of the hand already gripping the shotgun, pulled back my right arm, and said, "Sir, if you pick up that shotgun, I'm going to hit you in the face. I love you, Brother, and I want you to get saved, but I am not going to let you shoot us." He stormed away, and we had prayer with the wife and left.

I resigned that particular church to attend the seminary, but when my wife and I married, we attended that church the day after our wedding. This was about a year after that incident. We walked in while services were in progress, and I looked over to my left and there was that man. After the service, he, his wife, and daughters came up to me, and his little girl blurted out, "Brother Bailey, Daddy just got saved." They all embraced each other as we all wept and he said, "I'm sorry about . . . ." I said, "Brother, don't apologize. I'm so glad you belong to Jesus now."

Let our churches stand up and be places not committed to protecting a cultural image or cold form, but let us make them places so alive with the power of the living God that lost people feel the urgency of being born again when they walk into our buildings. Let the pulpit ring out the sweet, sweet song of salvation and warn the sinners of the error of their ways.

A lady said to a particular preacher, "You remind me of

my grandfather. He was one of the old hell-fire and brimstone preachers." Do you know what kind of a preacher that is? That's a Bible preacher, and God give us more of them!

The rural preacher prayed, "Lord, give me a backbone as big as a saw log and ribs like the sleepers under the church floor. Put iron shoes on me and galvanized britches. Give me a rhinoceros hide for skin and hang a wagon load of determination up in the gable end of my soul. Help me to sign a contract to fight the devil as long as I've got a fist, and then bite him as long as I've got a tooth, and then gum him until he dies."

The greatest message of the church is still: JESUS SAVES!

Have you considered what might be the only thing we can do on earth for Christ that we will not be able to do in heaven? I heard a man say the other day that the best thing is to praise Him. Oh, no. Revelation 7:12 says a gathering no man can number, dressed in white, will be saying, "Amen: Blessing, and glory, and wisdom, and thanksgiving, and honour, and power, and might, be unto our God for ever and ever. Amen."

You see, we can praise him in heaven, pray or talk to him in heaven, study his word in heaven, gather in his name in heaven, sing his songs and proclaim his victories, but we cannot witness there. That's why we must do it here.

That's why in Luke 15:7 Jesus said, "I say unto you, that likewise joy shall be in heaven over one sinner that repenteth, more than over ninety and nine just persons, which need no repentance." It's good we learn the Scriptures, attend seminars, conferences, institutes, and studies, but more than a reservoir of truth, we need to be rivers of blessing. When we stand before God someday, he will not ask us to quote Psalm 91. Instead, He will ask, "Whom did you bring with you?"

I recently heard the testimony of a man who had gone only to the eighth grade. He couldn't read well, and knew only

one verse in the Bible, but he had led 300 adult men and women to know Christ in two years. What good does it do to know if you do not share?

THE CHURCH WILL STAND UP FOR A CHRISTIAN AMERICA IN TODAY'S WORLD

Our nation was born, in part, during a prayer meeting on the Mayflower. The founding fathers wanted a place to bow before the living Christ. They wanted a place to establish religious freedom, but primarily Christian worship. The Bible was an open book. It was the first textbook in the schools. Our Constitution and Declaration of Independence were founded from the principles of a New Testament Church. We have placed "In God We Trust" on our money. On a particular postage stamp is a quote from the Bible, "Proclaim liberty thoughout all the land." Our schools were established to teach God's Word, and institutions of higher learning were founded by Christian men, many of them preachers.

Now, in today's world, one of these institutions recently heard an atheist at their invitation proclaim her Communist ideology, but refused to hear a renowned preacher of the gospel. Another such university gave a well-known agnostic a standing ovation as she bitterly denounced the God of heaven. But should we expect anything else when many of those students were reared in communities where no church has a strong Bible-believing, Spirit-filled, evangelistic voice? Students who went to schools where Christless teachers planted seeds of doubts and were influenced by a surrounding that has "deified man, humanized God, glorified sex, and liquorized society"? The Church of Jesus Christ wants a nation committed to her Lord that America's future might be as bright as her past.

I was talking recently with Dr. Bill Bright of Campus Crusade, and he said, "Bailey, I am convinced that unless there is

a wholesale turning to Christ this year, we will lose our nation. Last year 800,000 people in today's world lost their freedom. We could lose ours!"

Some say that 80 percent of our world now lives under dictatorship. We are almost the last stronghold of democracy. The church stands up for a free nation, and I am not sure we can remain free unless this nation indeed becomes more real in its Christianity. Remember, Jesus said that if the Son shall set you free, you shall be free indeed.

I want to share this lengthy word of Otto Whitaker:

I AM THE UNITED STATES

I was born on July 4th, 1776, and the Declaration of Independence is my birth certificate. The bloodliness of the world runs in my veins, because I offered freedom to the oppressed. I am many things, and many people—I AM THE UNITED STATES.

I am 190 million living souls—and the host of millions who have lived and died for me.

I am Nathan Hale and Paul Revere. I stood at Lexington and fired the shot heard around the world. I am Washington, Jefferson, and Patrick Henry. I am John Paul Jones, the Green Mountain boys, and Davy Crockett. I am Lee, Grant, and Abe Lincoln.

I remember the Alamo, the Maine, and Pearl Harbor. When freedom called, I answered and stayed until it was over, over there. I left my heroic dead in Flanders Field, on the rock of Corregidor, and on the bleak slopes of Korea.

I am the Brooklyn Bridge, the wheat lands of Kansas, and the granite hills of Vermont. I am the coal fields of the Virginias and Pennsylvania, the

fertile lands of the West, the Golden Gate and the Grand Canyon. I am Independence Hall, the Monitor, and the Merrimac.

I am big. I sprawl from the Atlantic to the Pacific, three million square miles throbbing with industry. I am more than five million farms. I am forest, field, mountain, and desert. I am quiet villages—and cities that never sleep. You can look at me and see Ben Franklin walking down the streets of Philadelphia with his bread loaf under his arm. You can see Betsy Ross with her needle. You can see the lights of Christmas, and hear the strains of "Auld Lang Syne" as the calendar turns.

I am Babe Ruth and the World Series. I am 169,000 schools and colleges, and 250,000 churches where my people worship God as they think best. I am a ballot dropped in a box, the roar of a crowd in a stadium, and the voice of a choir in a cathedral. I am an editorial in a newspaper, and a letter to a Congressman.

I am Eli Whitney and Stephen Foster. I am Tom Edison, Albert Einstein, and Billy Graham. I am Horace Greeley, Will Rogers, and the Wright Brothers. I am George Washington Carver, Daniel Webster, and Jonas Salk.

I am Longfellow, Harriet Beecher Stowe, Walt Whitman, and Thomas Paine. Yes, I am the Nation, and these are the things that I am. I was conceived in freedom and, God willing, in freedom will spend the rest of my days. May I possess always the integrity, the courage and the strength to keep myself unshackled, to remain a citadel of freedom and a beacon of hope to the world.

I AM THE UNITED STATES!

And it will always be the nation we love, free and joyful, as the church of God's Christ stands up and speaks up . . .

> Come world to Jesus, Come America to Jesus, and he will give you rest!

> God bless America, land that I love, Stand beside her, and guide her—

> Even so come, Lord Jesus!

13
Hour of Decision

Jesus loves you. Even though one may say no to him and curse him, he will still say, "I love you." There is nothing one can do to be unloved by God the Father and God the Son and God the Holy Ghost.

However, if one does not accept him in his mercy, one day that one will have to face him in his justice. He could not be God if he were not just. Justice simply means that justice *will* be done. The Bible promises that sin will be punished. That punishment is hell. Those who receive Christ are rewarded. That reward is heaven.

If you were to die tonight, where would you go? If you can say, "Preacher, I know that if I were to die tonight, I would go to heaven," that is a Christian testimony.

If you were to die tonight and you stood before God, and he said to you, "Why should I let you into heaven?" what would you say to him? You would probably say, "Well, I have been good. I have tried to be decent. I have been a good parent. I paid my bills. I have tried to be keeper of the Golden Rule and the Ten Commandments." If those are the things that are in your mind, it is a sure thing that you are not a Christian. The kind of person God will not save is the self-righteous person, the one who depends upon his own goodness.

He looked at the Pharisees and said, "You have closed the

door of damnation upon yourselves because the most righteous men in the world cannot get to heaven."

JESUS CHRIST OR SELF-RIGHTEOUSNESS

Only through Jesus Christ can you get to heaven. It is not bad people who go to hell and good people who go to heaven. It's saved people who go to heaven and lost people who go to hell.

The worst form of badness is human goodness substituted for the goodness of Jesus Christ. This is so because it places *your* righteousness and your goodness above the person of Jesus Christ. One just cannot do that.

Some are not worried about self-righteousness because they may be drunks or prostitutes. Jesus loves the dirtiest drunk in the gutter as much as he loves the man who sits behind the desk at the bank. He loves us all. He died for us all.

There are those who are miserable. Some have homes on the rocks. The reason for these problems is that Christ is not in the center of their lives. Christ is the only answer! If you were to enumerate your virtues to Christ, he would say, "Depart from me. I never knew you." But if you will look at God and say, "God, the only way I have to get to heaven is through the blood of Jesus Christ who died for me. I have accepted him," he will look at you and say, "Well done, good and faithful servant." At that point, you would enter heaven.

This life is brief. If one were to live 100 years, it would be only a brief time compared to eternity. Where are we going to live most of our real lives? It will be either in heaven or in hell. Which one will it be for you? One can't get to heaven by being a Baptist, a Church of Christ member, or a Catholic. One can get to heaven only by knowing he has made a personal commitment of his life to Jesus Christ.

Romans 10:13 says, "For whosoever shall call upon the name of the Lord shall be saved." If one were to ask Christ to save him right now, both God and I promise that he will. Re-

member, no one is saved by feelings, but by faith and by fact.

A person could think of so many things that he would first want to remove from his life. He might think he can be good enough to be saved. If the truth were known, not being good enough is the first prerequisite to being saved.

If the doctor gave you some medicine, you wouldn't take it home and put it on the dresser and wait until you were well to take it, would you? You would take the medicine in order to get well. My friend, whatever people are, Jesus can make them different. If they are dirty, he can make them pure. If they are lonely, he can keep them company. If they are weak, he can make them strong. If they are confused, he can get things straightened out in their lives. If they feel like they are downtrodden, Christ can put them on a mountaintop. If they know that inside of them their lives are hellish, he can make it heavenly. All one must do is invite him in. He has the answer! Whatever the problem or question is, he *is* the answer.

Pray this prayer silently in your heart, "Dear God, forgive me of my sins. I do want to be saved. I commit my life to Jesus Christ. Come into my heart right now, Jesus, and save me. Thank you, Jesus, for saving me right now."

When I was first called to preach, at the age of eighteen, I remember getting into the car on Sunday night. Dad would reach over to the radio and tune to Billy Graham's "Hour of Decision" program. My ears would get close to that radio because I knew God was working in my heart. Then Billy Graham would come on the radio, and he would say, "Ladies and gentlemen, I am going to preach tonight from coast to coast."

I would listen intently to Billy Graham. The first time I preached, I sounded just like Billy Graham. (A lot of young preachers have done that.) It is amazing how we want to copy those we admire. I would listen to that "Hour of Decision" so intently, because it was extremely vital for me to hear that man preach. He is a man gifted of God in so many ways. Other

team members do much of the preaching on that program now because of Billy Graham's schedule, but what an inspiration that program was and is to me.

Many of us face decisions. I heard of a preacher's wife who came home with a new dress. That preacher was not particularly Spirit-filled at the moment and said, "Honey, you know we can't afford a new dress. What did it cost?"

She replied, "It was on sale for $40. I just couldn't pass it up. I saved $20."

He said, "You didn't save $20—you spent $40. Why did you buy it?"

She said, "Well, the devil tempted me to buy it."

He said, "Why didn't you do what the Bible says and say, 'Get thee behind me, Satan' ?"

She said, "I did, but he said, 'It looks just as good from back here.' "

There are many decisions in life. Sometimes we encourage the devil to help us get what we want.

LOVE OF WORLD OR LOVE OF GOD

Look at Genesis 13:10-13:

> And Lot lifted up his eyes, and beheld all the plain of Jordan, that it was well watered everywhere, before the Lord destroyed Sodom and Gomorrah, even as the garden of the Lord, like the land of Egypt, as thou comest unto Zoar. Then Lot chose him all the plain of Jordan; and Lot journeyed east: and they separated themselves the one from the other. Abram dwelled in the land of Canaan, and Lot dwelled in the cities of the plain, and pitched his tent toward Sodom. But the men of Sodom were wicked and sinners before the Lord exceedingly.

What decision did Lot make? He made the decision for the world instead of God. That was his hour of decision.

First John 2:15 says, "Love not the world, neither the things that are in the world. If any man love the world, the love of the Father is not in him." Here is a man who came to a point of decision and made the wrong one!

He and Abraham decided to go in different directions. Abraham, the uncle of Lot, said, "Lot, you choose first." So Lot chose first and said, "I want the land of Jordan." He looked at the beautiful land of Jordan and saw how gorgeous it was. It was unbelievably green. The water would trickle through the valley as the rain would pour. I am sure that as he looked out from that Bethel plateau, he could not help but see the shimmering radiance of the morning sun as it glistened on that sparkling dew. I am sure he thought to himself, *What a fool I would be to choose the barren rocks of Judah, when I can have the fertile lands of Jordan.* Ths man began to compare the beautiful Jordan plains to the awful hills of Judah, and he chose that beautiful land.

There is nothing wrong with a man desiring a lovely home or wanting attractive gardens. God made things that are beautiful. There are very few pastimes that I enjoy more than driving through the Rockies and looking at Pikes Peak and seeing those beautiful Colorado spruce trees. Somehow we get the idea that the more spiritual we are, the more we have to be in love with the plain, mundane, unattractive things of life. That's not true! Some of the most dedicated Christians in the world have been lovers of that which is beautiful and lofty. We cannot condemn Lot for wanting the beautiful, fertile land compared to the barren rocks of Judah. There was nothing wrong with that choice.

The evil came about when God told him to go in the other direction. Where Lot wanted to go was truly a luscious land, but in the midst of all the beauty there was a snakebite. There was evil and corruption.

"What shall it profit a man if he gain the whole world, and lose his own soul?" Jesus called men who looked at the world

for possessions at the cost of their souls, "fools." Before we can consider material prosperity, we had better consider moral hazards. Before we consider financial returns, we had better consider spiritual corruption. I personally do not want to lose my life.

I have known women who would let their daughters do anything, if it would get them votes to be cheerleaders at the high school. If a parent is trying to push her daughter toward social graces, it could result in pushing them toward spiritual disgrace. There is nothing wrong with things that are beautiful and good, but in the midst of all of that, be careful. It is often true that in the most gorgeous foliage, there comes a snake that can kill. Be careful what kind of lessons you let your daughters take. That applies to sons as well. Dad, what do you want for your son?

One lady said, "Of course, I am letting my daughter go to cocktail parties. I want her to learn some of the finer graces of life."

Sometimes the choice is between the seemingly attractive. appealing things of the world and the better things of God. Often the choice is between things of the world and the superior things of Almighty God.

Lot became attracted to the surface considerations, and he forgot what was inside of that decision. Some are thinking about the big financial deal they are going to pull off. Now remember, there is nothing wrong with being wealthy. But if you have to sell your soul to do it, you will regret it as long as you live, in this life and the next. It is a shame that some people come to the hour of decision about the world and God, and make the wrong choice.

I have had people say, "We are so happy. We bought a cabin down at the lake. We can now go to the lake three weekends a month." That makes my heart weep. Sure, one needs to go somewhere occasionally, but we need to be careful what we invest in. It might be that we could obligate ourselves to something that will take our time to such a degree

that we will soon become spiritual pygmies. We will then be no good to God, his church, or anyone else—but the devil.

We will sap our spiritual strength. We must beware that we have the appealing things of the world fully considered before we choose. We might miss the deeper things of God.

Some parents become upset when their children are saved or when they come forward to surrender for the ministry. The parents wanted "something better" for that child.

I would rather my boys be missionaries, die at the bloody hands of savages in the foreign jungles, and love God, than graduate from Oxford and go to parties with big shots that put a doubt over the Word. I have no financial ambitions for my children—only spiritual ambitions. If we live in a shack with Jesus in our hearts, we are kings. What will a man give in exchange for his soul? The hour of decision is now.

BELIEVING GOD OR DOUBTING GOD

Numbers 13:31-33 says:

> But the men that went up with him said, We be not able to go up against the people; for they are stronger than we. And they brought up an evil report of the land which they had searched unto the children of Israel, saying, The land, through which we have gone to search it, is a land that eateth up the inhabitants thereof; and all the people that we saw in it are men of a great stature. And there we saw the giants, the sons of Anak, which come of the giants: and we were in our own sight as grasshoppers, and so we were in their sight.

In the case of the children of Israel their hour of decision was between believing God and doubting God. God told them to conquer the land and the land would belong to Israel. Joshua and Caleb went to spy the land out. They came back and said, "We can do it. There are only two of us who believe that, but we can do it." However, the majority of the spies

said, "We can't do it. We are like grasshoppers compared to them."

God had already promised them the land. The reason some churches stay dry is because they believe their brain instead of God. If I had to depend on this brain, I would be in a bad shape. When a person believes God and makes a decision toward God, that's the issue.

Do you remember when the Israelites faced the giant named Goliath? They had their armor and swords, but they wouldn't fight that giant for anything. But then, here came a little shepherd boy who reached down and picked up five rocks. He put one in a slingshot and toppled the giant with the first shot. The Israelites thought the giant was too big to hit, but David thought he was too big to miss. That's the difference. It is a matter of believing God.

God has told us to witness. God has told us to tithe. God has told us to be faithful. God has told us to pray. God has told us to be preachers. But some won't heed God's word. Some are letting the insanity of their human rationale be more influential in their lives than the Word of God.

We face giants all the time. The body is the temple of the Holy Spirit. We don't have to be afraid when God tells us to do something. God never told us to do anything that he will let us do alone.

David's rock knocked that giant down because there was a giant torpedo following it. When we get ourselves in line with God, God will bring us power that we never dreamed of. Are we making the decision of whether to believe God or not to believe God? The rest of the spies said, "I know what God said, but we still don't think we can do that."

HUMAN LOGIC OR OBEDIENCE TO GOD

First Samuel 15:23 says, "For rebellion is as the sin of witchcraft, and stubbornness is as iniquity and idolatry. Because thou hast rejected the word of the Lord, he hath also rejected thee from being king."

Saul was a man who had never fulfilled his greatest spiritual heights because he decided to do what he wanted to do instead of what God wanted him to do. He had to make the decision between human logic and being obedient to the things of God. Israel was afraid. They questioned God. But Saul disobeyed God at every turn.

Many people tell me they do not like hearing sermons on hell because they conjure up terrible thoughts. What do you think hell is? It *is* terrible! It is hell.

A lady once said, "To me, God is a loving, understanding, merciful God." And that's true, but that's half of the coin. He is also a God of judgment and justice. This is exactly what Saul was thinking when he disobeyed. He said, "God, I know what you said, but. . . ."

There are some we talk to about being saved, and they will say, "I've been good." Oh, the number of "good people" who are going to burn in hell!

Quit trying to write the Bible. It has already been written. God doesn't want us to take what we believe and throw out what we don't want to believe. The Bible stands as it is. There are some people who always say, "I know what the Bible says, but. . . ." My friend, that little conjunction can send you straight to hell.

Some think they are intelligent and brilliant scholarly and don't want to "waste their brilliant minds" on being a preacher. "If one has intelligence, he certainly should be a doctor or lawyer. A man with a brain wouldn't want to be a preacher!" some people claim. But, if God is telling you to preach, you had better listen! When God speaks, one shouldn't try to put an amendment to his Word. He doesn't want an addendum to what he is saying. When God speaks, he means for us to obey.

There are those who say, "Well, Preacher, I have this little sin, but I know God doesn't begrudge one little sin."

Well, first of all, there is no little sin. Second, Jesus says, "Be ye perfect even as your Father in heaven is perfect." God

does begrudge that little sin. Then there are others who say, "Well, I know what the Bible says about being faithful, but I work six days a week. On the seventh day I just feel like I should keep that day for me." If we know what the Bible teaches, and we don't follow it, we are in dire danger. The Bible clearly teaches that he who knows to do good and does it not, to him it is sin (see James 4:17). If we know what the Bible says, and we don't respond to it, we are in danger of the judgment of God.

What decision did Saul make? Whether to believe God or believe his own logic.

TO BE RELIGIOUS OR TO BE CHRISTIAN

Matthew 23:38 says, "Behold, your house is left unto you desolate." There are none so blind as those who will not see. Here the Pharisees refused to see. What was their hour of decision? Their hour of decision was over whether to be religious or to be Christian. One of the worst dangers in the world is religious fervor that is substituted for the spirit and for the life of Jesus Christ.

Jesus looked at those Pharisees who prayed and memorized Scriptures, and said, "Your life is empty." Their decision was whether to be religious or Christian. A Christian is not a person who does many things for Jesus. A Christian is a person who looks like Jesus. I have known some of the meanest men in the world to be on a church staff. They were active and busy, but they had the spirit of the devil in them. I have known deacons the same way. Jesus said, "Your house is left unto you desolate." Some people need to ask themselves if they have been more religious than Christian.

TRUST JESUS OR ONE'S OWN POSSESSIONS

Mark 10:21-22 says:

> Then Jesus beholding him loved him, and said unto him, One thing thou lackest: go thy way, sell what-

soever thou hast, and give to the poor, and thou shalt have treasure in heaven: and come, take up the cross, and follow me. And he was sad at that saying, and went away grieved: for he had great possessions.

What decision did this young man make? His hour of decision was whether he could trust Jesus or not trust Jesus. We do not mean trust Jesus as personal Lord and Savior. We mean trust him like we would have to trust a person if we were to jump off a building into their arms.

Jesus said to the rich young ruler, "Look, in order for you to get what you want, you must sell everything you have and give to the poor." To which he replied, "God, you don't understand. Look at everything I have. I have great possessions. I am a man of huge investments. I am a man who has a good income." Jesus never looked at him and said, "Well, I didn't understand that. Oh well, you can come on anyway." Jesus let him turn and walk away.

Here's the point. He didn't trust Jesus. I believe that this man said to Jesus, "Lord, what do you want me to do? Sell everything I have and give to the poor?" "Yes," said Jesus. If he had bowed on his knees before Christ and said, "Master, if that is what you want me to do, I'll do it," I believe Jesus would have looked at him and said, "Well, if you will, you don't have to."

The only way we can keep what we have is to be willing to give it up. The only way we can gain is to lose it all. That's the only way. God wants to know that we trust him with all our hearts. He wants us to trust him with all of our problems. There are none too small or too large. He wants us to come just like we are. Come out from that old life and watch him do some miracles.

TRUSTING JESUS TO HANDLE PROBLEMS

For some the hour of decision is, "Do I really trust Jesus enough to believe that he can handle my problems?"

When a man comes to know Jesus Christ, he gets on the receiving side. We receive. A person who brags about how much he had to give up to get Jesus, never got Jesus. A person knows that when he comes to Jesus, he becomes richer and the wealthier because of it. The hour of decision might simply be, "Do you trust Jesus with your needs and problems?"

RECEIVE CHRIST NOW OR LATER

Acts 24:25 says, "And as he reasoned of righteousness, temperance, and judgment to come, Felix trembled, and answered, Go thy way for this time; when I have a convenient season, I will call for thee."

I have heard that. "Don't call me—I'll call you." Felix's hour of decision was whether to be saved then or delay. There is no record in the Bible where anyone ever turned Jesus down who later accepted him. There is no evidence in the Scripture that anyone who said *no* to Christ, accepted Him the next week. As far as we know, Felix is in hell right now. He came to his hour of decision and said, "No, not now."

God is not some kind of carhop at the root-beer stand. We cannot call him when we want him.

God said, "No man can come to me except the Father which hath sent me draw him." Seek the Lord while he may be found. Felix thought tomorrow might be fine.

One man once said, "Preacher, I think I am just too lazy to be saved." Numerous people never become Christians because they don't have high enough standards to appreciate what Jesus has to offer. They are like the hogs. Many don't have love for Jesus because they have such a low level of desire for life. The things of evil and rottenness appeal to their demented minds. Here was a man who said he was too lazy.

I have had women say to me, "I am waiting for my husband." What will they say when they wait too long and awake in hell? We had better not wait on anyone. We had better re-

spond when the Holy Spirit woos us. Felix said, "Some other time." Some are going to make the decision of whether or not to delay.

God has no responsibility for you ever to hear the gospel again. He is under no obligation for you to hear his Word again. This may be the last time. This is your moment—your hour of decision!